Wishing you a future of
family harmony!
Cameron

POWER PHRASES *for Parents:* TEEN EDITION

Cameron L. Caswell, Ph.D.

ISBN: 978-1-4834-2620-4 (sc)
ISBN: 978-1-4834-2619-8 (e)

Library of Congress Control Number: 2015902088

Lulu Publishing Services rev. date: 03/03/2015

I dedicate this book to
my mom, Sherrill, for her continuous love and support,
and my daughter, Alexa, for inspiring me to be a better parent every day.

Contents

Introduction

Communication is the backbone to any relationship. Unfortunately, communication between parents and teens frequently breaks down, causing frustration, misunderstanding, resentment and stress.

This communication collapse often occurs because an adolescent's brain processes and interprets information differently from an adult's. Adults look at things through a logical lens, while emotions color the perception of teens. Teens can't help it; their prefrontal cortex (the part of the brain that controls reasoning and logic) won't fully develop until well into their twenties. Until then, you and your teen are basically speaking different languages.

Teens are also biologically driven to seek autonomy and question authority as they work on defining their individuality. Their quest for independence butts up against their parents' reluctance to relinquish control, and suddenly they find themselves on opposing sides. As teens and their parents both hold steadfast to their own expectations, while pushing the other to change, they find themselves in power struggle after power struggle. Ending this vicious cycle requires taking responsibility for the part YOU play and changing your approach.

To help, I've provided more than a thousand power phrases designed to keep your message brief and clear, establish authority, exude understanding, and build your teen's trust in you. Select your favorites, tweak them so they sound more like you, then work them into your daily interactions with your teen. Combine the words with a cool, calm demeanor and a willingness to listen and watch as the power struggles amazingly transform into powerful connections.

Here's to finding family harmony.

How to Use This Book

Let's face it; conflict with your teen is inevitable. And when it occurs, how often have you struggled to find the appropriate thing to say? When you have the right words and phrases at your command, you can handle even the most challenging situations with poise and grace, and quickly resolve issues before they spiral out of control.

Power Phrases for Parents: Teen Edition puts the right words at your fingertips. The first several categories are general and can be easily modified to fit just about any situation. The rest are geared toward specific topics and have been crafted to provide the essential information that your teen needs to make smart choices and handle difficult situations with confidence. It is important to note that the suggested phrases are grounded in scientific research, developmental theory and basic legal guidelines. They are not intended to reflect specific religious beliefs or cultural values.

How to Use Power Phrases:

1. Select the phrase that best fits your situation, your child's age and maturity level, and your personality.
2. Personalize the phrase by inserting the suggested information (e.g., <emotion>), much like you would a *Mad Lib*, and ensure that it reflects your family's religious beliefs and values.
3. Tweak the words to make the phrase sound like you and practice it so that you sound natural and sincere.
4. Believe in it. For the words to be effective, you must say them with authority. To speak with authority, you must truly believe in what you're saying. Teens have a very powerful BS detector, so they'll know if you're not speaking from a place of truth.
5. Follow through with what you say.

Did You Know?

Rather than waiting to have one big, often-awkward, talk, it is best to disperse information and ask questions a little at a time throughout their childhood and adolescence.

Talking Tip

If you or your teen is particularly uncomfortable or resistant to talking about a specific topic, try writing a note highlighting your thoughts and giving it to her to read. Once your teen has read it, ask her if she has any questions or concerns about the topic.

Talking to Teens Checklist

How do you become the type of parent your teen trusts and wants to talk to? It's all in your approach.

- ❑ **Listen more. Talk less.** The main reason teens don't like talking to parents is because they "will not shut up." When you talk with your teen, focus on being present, staying silent and paying attention.
- ❑ **Lose the lectures.** No matter how wise your words may be, your teen will reflexively tune you out as soon as he senses a lecture coming on. Chances are he'll avoid coming to you in the future too.
- ❑ **Enlist yourself as an ally.** There may be times (a lot of them), when your teen feels like the entire world is against her. More than ever she needs to know that you are on her side.
- ❑ **Persist, but don't push.** Your teen is more likely to talk to you when the conversation is on his terms. Let your teen know that you're always there to listen, and continue to drop gentle reminders until he's ready.
- ❑ **Be interruptible.** When your teen finally does decide that she wants to talk, prove to her that she's a priority by giving her your undivided attention.
- ❑ **Pick the right time and place.** Select a time when both of you are feeling calm and unhurried. Find a place that has few distractions and as much privacy as possible.
- ❑ **Collect conversation fuel.** Compile a list of fun topics and thought-provoking questions that can spark small talk (see the Conversation Fuel Cheat Sheet for suggestions). The more comfortable that the two of you get talking about "nothing," the easier it'll be when you have to talk about something serious.

Did You Know?

The number one wish for most teen girls is that their parents would talk to them more openly and frequently.[1]

Communication Kryptonite

"Whatever words we utter should be chosen with care for people will hear them and be influenced by them for good or ill." —The Buddha

Many parents resort to the following tactics in an attempt to exert their authority and control their teen. More often than not, these tactics backfire, causing teens to act out, shut down, fight back, and give up. If you want to earn and keep your teen's respect, steer clear of:

1. **Blaming.** Sure, your teen may have done something wrong — broken a rule or acted inappropriately — but you'll crush any opportunity for him to learn from his mistake if you provoke him to become defensive by accusing or blaming him outright. This may also prompt him to lie in an attempt to avoid getting into more trouble.

   <u>What to do instead</u>: Model accountability by taking control of your own reaction and attitude. Teach your teen how to take responsibility for his actions by telling him how you feel about his negative behavior and explaining what you like or expect from him in the future. Then listen to his side of the story and help steer him toward a more acceptable solution for the future.

2. **Criticizing.** When teens mess up, parents often jump to point out their mistake all too quickly. It's important to steer your teen in the right direction, but in a way that doesn't come across as a personal attack. The only thing criticizing and shaming your teen will do is chip away at her already fragile self-esteem and erode her trust in you.

   <u>What to do instead</u>: It's up to you to help her identify what went wrong and find solutions. This is best done with constructive feedback; however it's often difficult to distinguish between that and criticism. A good rule of thumb is to focus on the specific behavior or incident that you're unhappy with (e.g., a bad grade on

this week's science test), rather than attacking your teen's character with a sweeping generalization like "You're so lazy" or "What the hell is wrong with you?" Keep in mind, the ultimate goal is to teach her how to distinguish between good and bad decisions.

3. **Lecturing.** Oh how parents love to turn every possible moment into a teaching moment. The problem is, the conversation usually ends up being one-sided, with the parents droning on and on and the teen tuning them out — no matter how wise their words may be.

   What to do instead: Talk less (far less) and listen more. Ask open-ended questions to keep your teen talking and to help him come to his own conclusions. He'll walk away amazed at how helpful and understanding you are, and will also be more likely to come to you the next time he needs help.

4. **Nagging.** Sometimes it feels like you're stuck on a constant loop, repeating the same comment over and over: "Did you do your homework?" "Did you do your homework?" "Did you do your homework?" In the end, you feel frustrated and angry, your teen is annoyed and bitter, and the homework *still* isn't done.

   What to do instead**:** Rather than remind your teen 100 times to do her homework, spell out what you expect her to do — just once. Briefly explain what will happen if she doesn't complete the task, then leave it alone. For example, "You cannot talk on the phone until your homework is completed." Now the ball is in your teen's court and it's her choice to either complete her homework and earn the privilege to talk on the phone, or to skip her homework and lose her phone for the evening.

5. **Name-calling, swearing, and threatening**. Parents who discipline their teenagers by cursing, threatening, and name-calling, or in other words, by bullying, may ultimately be doing far more harm

than good. In fact, this form of verbal abuse actually has been shown to promote teen misbehavior rather than reduce it. For example, numerous studies have found associations between harsh parenting (spanking, threatening, yelling, grabbing, verbal coercion) and higher rates of defiance, behavior problems, depression and anxiety.

<u>What to do instead</u>: Remember the adage, "If you don't have anything nice to say, don't say anything at all"? It's a good one.

6. **Sarcasm**. While humor and gentle teasing may strengthen your relationship with your teen, sarcasm will more likely strain it. You may think what you're saying is funny, but teens often translate words literally and may perceive your sarcasm as hurtful, callous, and even outright cruel. You may think *your* teen gets your sarcastic wit, but are you willing to risk your teen's confidence in you over a clever little jab?

   <u>What to do instead</u>**:** If it's too good to keep to yourself, wait and share it with someone who doesn't count on your emotional support so much.

7. **Stonewalling**. Parents sometimes try to convey their disapproval by ignoring their teen or giving him "the silent treatment." Although it may seem harmless, your teen may perceive it as uncaring or indifference toward him. Additionally, shutting your teen out doesn't help resolve the problem or build your teen's trust.

   <u>What to do instead</u>**:** If you need to take a moment to gather your thoughts or regain your composure, then say so instead of walking away in silence. Give yourself about 20 minutes or so to pull yourself together, then restart the conversation.

8. **Yelling**. When your teen starts pushing your buttons, yelling is often a natural response. Unfortunately, every time you "lose it" and yell, scream or give an overly harsh punishment, you undermine your authority by

showing her that you aren't really in control. Also, instead of forcing your teen to listen, your loud voice acts as an aversive stimulus, which your teen will instinctually tune out and ignore. Once your teen shuts down, your message has no chance of getting through to her.

What to do instead**:** The only way you can be assured that you are effectively communicating with your teen is if your emotions are under control. Staying calm and level-headed also increases your credibility and authority and earns your teen's respect. If you feel the urge to yell, put yourself on a 'time out' until you have better control.

If (or rather, when) you do slip up and resort to using communication kryptonite with your teen, the best way to turn things around is to apologize. Many parents fear that admitting they messed up will undermine their authority, but it does just the opposite. It helps you model humility, respect and accountability — characteristics that are important to instill in your child. It also shows your teen that it's OK to make mistakes and provides him with an example of how to make an effective apology. In the end, your teen will only respect and trust you more.

Talking Tip

If you frequently use one or more of the communication killers above, set a goal to minimize it. Once you break your bad habit, your interactions with your teen will go much more smoothly.

Personal Goal

The conversation killer I want to stop using is ________________________.

The next time I get the urge to ________________________________,
I'll bite my tongue and listen instead.

20 Power Phrases to Address Your Teen's Disrespect

(Back Talk, Defiance and Sass)

"Nothing is more despicable than respect based on fear." —Albert Camus

1. Can you think of a different way to answer me so I can be clear about what you really want?
2. Hear me out, and I will do the same for you.
3. How would you treat a good friend in this same situation?
4. I don't deserve to be insulted like that—no one does. This conversation is over until we can both be more respectful of one another.
5. I don't know if you realize it, but when you <insert behavior> it <consequences>. Can you think of a more effective way to approach this?
6. I don't like hearing put-downs in our family. If you want <request>, then I expect you to say it in a way that won't hurt someone's feelings.
7. I feel <insert emotion> when you <behavior>. To avoid losing my cool, I'm going to walk away. Let me know when you're ready to talk nicely.
8. I get upset when someone walks out on me when I'm still talking. If what I'm saying bothers you, just tell me and I'll listen.
9. I love you, but I don't appreciate your attitude right now. I'll be happy to discuss this with you when we can each be respectful of one another.
10. I want to hear your point as soon as I've completed mine.
11. I will always love you no matter what, but I can't accept <behavior> because <reason>. What would you do if you were me?
12. I'd appreciate it if you lowered your voice. I want to make sure I hear everything you have to say, but I can't focus when you talk that way.
13. I'm happy to help whenever I can, but it'd mean a lot to me if you showed me some appreciation.
14. I'm having trouble listening to you when you speak to me like this.

15. It'd really help me understand what you need if you'd come right out and tell me how you're feeling. Are you angry? Frustrated? Sad?
16. Please allow me to complete my point and then you can make yours.
17. Please, hold that thought until I've completed mine. Thank you.
18. Right now, you're coming across as disrespectful. I understand that you're feeling <emotion>, but there are better ways to handle it. Do you need a few minutes to come up with a different approach?
19. What you just said really hurt my feelings.
20. When you <behavior> I feel <emotion>. Is that your intention?

Did You Know?

The only thing excessive questioning, lectures, nagging, yelling, and criticism will get you is more anger, resentment, stubbornness, opposition, and back talk from your teen. You have the power to stop the cycle of disrespect.

Talking Tip

To earn your teen's respect, remember to:

- Act with integrity.
- Be confident but humble.
- Be firm but fair.
- Be kind.
- Keep your word.
- Listen and learn.
- Respect yourself and others.
- Stay calm.

Related Tools

- Behavior Agreement

Related Chapters

- Buy More Time to Respond
- Challenge a Sense of Entitlement
- Confront a Teen Who's Lying
- Cool Down a Heated Situation
- Enforce Rules and Consequences
- Respond to Arguing
- Say "No" with Authority
- Extreme Emotions

7 Power Phrases to Buy More Time to Respond

"Speak when you are angry—and you'll make the best speech you'll ever regret." —Laurence J. Peter

1. I am not convinced one way or another. I'll give you an answer by ...
2. I don't know, but I'll find out and get back to you as soon as possible.
3. I know this is important to you, so I don't want to make a rash decision. I'll have an answer by ...
4. I need more time to think about this so that I can give you a fair answer. I'll let you know by ...
5. I'll need to get more information before I make my final decision.
6. I need some time to process what you just told me. Let's talk about this some more at ...
7. Unfortunately, I don't have the time to give this the attention it deserves right now. I'll get back to you with an answer by ...

Did You Know?

It's best to buy some time if:

- You are overly emotional, or your teen is.
- You are too distracted to focus.
- You need to get more information.
- You want your teen to try to solve the problem herself.

Talking Tip

Make an appointment. Provide a specific date and/or time to continue the discussion rather than leaving it open-ended.

27 Power Phrases to Boost Your Teen's Self-Esteem

(The Right Way to Praise)

"My parents are my backbone. Still are. They're the only group that will support you if you score zero or you score 40." —Kobe Bryant

1. I admire <quality> about you.
2. I am deeply impressed by <insert behavior> because ...
3. I am in awe of your ability to ...
4. I am proud of you for ...
5. I appreciate the time and thought you put into ...
6. I can tell you have an excellent sense of <skill> because ...
7. I can tell you spent a lot of time thinking this through.
8. I know it was difficult to <task>, but you did it.
9. I see your attention to detail in how you ...
10. I was impressed by how you ...
11. I'm amazed at the incredible person you're becoming.
12. I'm in awe of your ability to . . .
13. I've noticed you've really improved at <skill>. What have you been doing to get better?
14. It looks like you put a lot of work into this.
15. It's clear from your results that you have been working very hard.
16. Now that's what I call ...
17. Now you've got it.
18. Sorry I haven't told you recently just how proud I am of you. Keep up the good work.
19. That's amazing. I'd love it if you taught me how you ...
20. When you did <task>, it made my job easier because ...
21. Wow! Your hard work is paying off.
22. You handled <situation> beautifully.
23. You have always done things when you were ready for them, not on anyone else's agenda. Keep being true to yourself!

24. You must be proud of yourself for ...
25. You seem to be a natural at ...
26. You're getting good at <skill>. That must feel really good.
27. Your performance at the <event> was incredible. Let's go out tonight and celebrate.

Did You Know?

Common sense guides us to praise our teen every chance we get to build up his self-esteem. But studies show that pumping your child full of unwarranted praise can actually do more harm than good. Shielding your teen from failure, running interference for him, and creating artificial success experiences all have a negative impact on his self-esteem. The key to effective praise is to be genuine, sincere and specific. Try praising your teen by telling him what you observed, how much you liked/loved it and why.

Talking Tip

Teens will always discount what their parents say—you're their parents, you're supposed to say that. To increase the impact of your praise, catch your teen doing something right. Even better, let your teen overhear you saying something positive about her to someone else.

Quick Trick

10 Ways to Improve Self-Esteem

1. Appreciate your strengths and accept your weaknesses.
2. Do the best you can in each moment.
3. Do the things that make you happy.
4. Don't compare yourself to others.
5. Focus on your well-being—exercise, eat healthy foods, manage your stress.
6. Make a difference—volunteer, pay it forward, be nice to everyone.

7. Set realistic goals for yourself and celebrate your achievements.
8. Trust your own feelings, opinions, and ideas.
9. Try to stop thinking negative thoughts about yourself.
10. View your mistakes as learning opportunities rather than beating yourself up about them.

Related Chapters

- Comfort Your Teen
- Give Constructive Feedback
- Make Your Teen Feel Valued
- Say "I Love You"
- Promote a Positive Body Image

19 Power Phrases to Challenge a Sense of Entitlement

"The world does not owe you a living; you owe the world something. You owe it your time, energy and talent. Develop a backbone, not a wishbone....You are important, and you are needed."
—John Tapene, Principal, Northland College (1959)

1. Do you believe you worked just as hard, if not harder, than everyone else? How so?
2. I can give you a budget of $_____ for ... You are responsible for covering anything over that, so you may want to prioritize the things you really need and want.
3. I get it. It's pretty disappointing to do your best and still not win, especially when you wanted it so much. But you know, you haven't really earned it yet. There are a lot of other kids that have been doing this longer and practicing even harder than you. If this is something you really want, then you're going to have to put even more effort into it. However, if you want to do this just for fun, that's fine too. You just can't expect to win without dedicating yourself fully to it.
4. I know it means a lot to you. I am willing to give you $______ toward it—the rest you can either work for or take from your allowance.
5. I understand that you really want ... Perhaps you can buy it with your birthday money.
6. I want to help you earn some money because I know you really want ... I also could use some extra help around the house. I'll pay you $______ if you complete <task>.
7. I'd love for you to do that too. What is your plan to earn that privilege?
8. I'm sorry. There are going to be some disappointments in life and this is one of them. Do you want to talk about it?
9. If you want it badly enough, I'm confident you'll find a way to earn it.

10. It's not how <talented/smart/etc.> you are that matters, it's how dedicated and tenacious you are that counts. That's what makes people successful.
11. I'm willing to loan you $_____. What do you have for collateral?
12. That's a lofty goal. You're going to have to work really hard to achieve it, but I believe you have the perseverance to succeed.
13. What's your plan of action to reach your goal? How can I help?
14. Who is someone you admire? Let's look online and find out how they got to where they are. I'm guessing they had to overcome a lot of obstacles to get there.
15. Why do you feel like you deserve it more than anyone else?
16. Why do you think you were treated unfairly?
17. How much is it? That's just ____ weeks of allowance. Start saving now and you'll have enough to buy it in ____ weeks.
18. You said you wanted ________ also. I can get you one or the other. Which is more essential?
19. You should put that on your Christmas wish list.

Did You Know?

Materialism—a value system based on wealth, status, image, and material consumption—is directly related to a lack of happiness and satisfaction.[2]

Talking Tip

6 ways to teach teens to "learn to earn":

1. Encourage … volunteering INSTEAD OF shopping.
2. Focus on … effort INSTEAD OF winning.
3. Foster … gratitude INSTEAD OF greed.
4. Give … opportunities to earn INSTEAD OF everything they want.
5. Reward with … your attention INSTEAD OF material goods.
6. Send … thank you notes INSTEAD OF wish lists.

Related Tools

- Curfew Agreement
- Dating Agreement
- Homework Agreement
- Household Responsibilities Agreement

Related Chapters

- Address Disrespect
- Encourage Accountability
- Prompt Your Teen to Problem-Solve
- Spark Collaboration
- Teach Money Management
- Discourage Underachievement

15 Power Phrases to Clarify the Facts

(Reflective Listening)

"Any man who can drive safely while kissing a pretty girl is simply not giving the kiss the attention it deserves." —Albert Einstein

1. Are you saying that …?
2. By that you mean …?
3. Correct me if I'm wrong, but what I hear you saying is …
4. I get the impression that <observation>. Is that correct?
5. I may not understand you correctly, and I find myself taking what you said personally. What I thought you just said is … Is that what you meant?
6. I think I see where you're coming from. You're saying that … Is that right?
7. If I understand correctly, you're saying that …
8. I'm getting the impression that <observation>. Am I close?
9. It sounds like you …
10. On a scale from 1 to 10, how <emotion> are you feeling? What makes it a <number>?
11. So what you're getting at is ...?
12. So what you're saying is <summarize>. Yes?
13. What exactly do you mean when you say…?
14. What I hear you say is that you feel <emotion> and you want …
15. What I thought you said is <summarize>. Is that what you meant?

Did You Know?

To a teen, being understood is everything. Reflective listening is not only one of the best ways to show your teen that you care but is a powerful way to defuse his explosive emotions. In fact, professionals such as police officers, emergency medical technicians, and call center agents, all of whom need to calm people down quickly to get to the facts, also use this technique.

Talking Tip

To listen reflectively, try:

1. Listening to your teen without judgment, even if you don't agree with what she's saying.
2. Summarizing in your own words what your teen said.
3. Asking clarifying questions to verify what your teen is feeling, such as, "Are you saying that …?"

Related Chapters

- Coax Your Teen to Open Up to You
- Confront a Teen Who's Lying
- Prevent Misunderstandings

43 Power Phrases to Coax Your Teen to Open Up to You

(Open-Ended Questions)

"When people talk, listen completely. Most people never listen." —Ernest Hemingway

1. Can you tell me more about …?
2. Do you want to talk about it?
3. Have I done something to upset you?
4. Have you felt this way before?
5. How did you come to this conclusion?
6. How did you feel when …?
7. How do you feel about that?
8. How so?
9. I appreciate your desire to keep your feelings private, but if there is anything I can do to help, let me know.
10. I don't like having unspoken issues between us. Can we clear the air?
11. I know I can't fix it, but I can listen.
12. I know in the past I may not have done a good job of listening to you. I want to do better this time if you'll let me try.
13. I like the way you <insert action>. Can you tell/show me how you did that?
14. I must not fully understand what's going on. I want to. I'll keep listening as long as it takes.
15. I'd like to help you, but I only can do that if you talk to me. Let me know when you're ready, and I'll listen.
16. Is something bothering you? I know you don't think I'll understand, but I'd like to try.
17. I've noticed a change in your mood. Is there something going on?
18. I've noticed your interest in <interest>. I'd love to hear about it.

19. If you don't want to tell me something because you think I'll be disappointed in you, please know that's not the case. I will still support you no matter what you tell me.
20. If you ever feel like you can't tell me something because you're worried that I can't handle it, I want to reassure you that I can. There is nothing more important to me than you and our family.
21. Is there anything going on that you think I should know?
22. Is there anything that you need from me?
23. Let me know if there is anything that I can do to support you.
24. Not many people would be willing to talk about this. I love how honest you are being right now.
25. Please know that I'm here to listen to you anytime that you'd like to talk.
26. Sometimes you and I have a difficult time together. How do you feel about that?
27. Tell me more about …
28. Thanks for sharing that. I wondered how teenagers see that issue.
29. That sounds important to you. I'd love to hear more about it.
30. That sounds interesting. Can you tell me more?
31. Then what happened?
32. Want to <go for a walk/grab a cup of coffee/etc.>?
33. What can I do to help you with ...?
34. What do you think?
35. What does that mean to you?
36. What kind of help do you need?
37. What was the real issue?
38. What would you like to see happen?
39. Whenever you're ready to share, I'm ready to listen.
40. Why do you think she did that?
41. Would you like to share more about that?
42. You got really quiet when I mentioned … Why is that?
43. You've been <emotion> lately. Want to share what's on your mind?

Did You Know?

51 percent of teens are afraid to talk to their parents about personal problems.[3]

Talking Tip

One of the most powerful ways to get your teen to open up to you is to ask a simple, open-ended question, which requires more than a one-word answer. Then let him talk while you listen intently.

Quick Trick

To ensure that you have all the facts, ask the 5 "W's":

1. Who? (Who are you going with? Who's driving?)
2. What? (What will you be doing?)
3. Where? (Where are you going?)
4. When? (When will you be home?)
5. Why? (Why is this important to you?)

Related Chapters

- Clarify the Facts
- Confront a Teen Who's Lying
- Spark Collaboration

31 Power Phrases to Comfort Your Teen

(Empathy and Understanding)

"A prerequisite to empathy is simply paying attention to the person in pain."
—Daniel Goldman

1. I can hear how <emotion> you're feeling right now.
2. I can only begin to imagine how much that would <hurt you, bother you, make you mad, etc.>.
3. I can see how important this is to you.
4. I can't imagine how upsetting it is to …
5. I don't blame you for feeling <insert emotion> about …
6. I hear you say that you're feeling ...
7. I sense that you are feeling <emotion> right now, and that's OK.
8. I think I can see where you're coming from.
9. I think I understand what you're feeling. I often felt that way when I was your age, too.
10. I understand. If that happened to me, I'd feel <emotion> too.
11. I wonder if you're feeling ...
12. I'm sorry you've had such a bad experience. Is there anything I can do to help?
13. I'm so sorry to hear that.
14. I'm sorry you feel that way.
15. I'm sorry you're feeling <emotion> about <situation>. How can I help?
16. It seems like you're feeling ...
17. It sounds like you're <emotion> about <situation>. Is that what you're feeling?
18. It sounds to me like you are really feeling …
19. It's perfectly understandable that you're <emotion> about what happened.
20. It's OK to feel <emotion> about ...

21. That must have been really <adjective>. Do you want to talk about it?
22. That must really feel bad to you.
23. What would make you feel better?
24. When I look at this from your viewpoint, what you're saying makes sense to me.
25. When I put myself in your shoes, I can see why you would feel that way.
26. You have every right to feel <emotion>. I'm here if you want me to listen.
27. You may start to feel a need to pull away from me during this time. That's OK. This is your time to discover who you are, independent of me. Just know that I love you and I'll always be here for you when you want to talk or have someone to lean on.
28. You must be feeling <emotion>. Are you all right?
29. You must be feeling pretty …
30. You seem to be feeling <emotion> about <situation>. I would too.
31. You sound really <emotion>, but I'm not sure why. Would you like to talk about it?

Did You Know?

It may seem like your teen is constantly pushing you away, but she really does want (and need) your love and support—especially when she's hurting. It's not going to be easy for her to reach out to you, though, so you'll need to make the first move. Talking with your teen frequently about mundane, day-to-day experiences also will make her feel more comfortable asking for your help in more-serious situations.

Talking Tip

The best way to comfort your teen is to:

- Listen.

- Validate his feelings.
- Not try to fix it.
- Listen some more.

Quick Trick

One of the easiest, most effective ways to convey empathy is to match your teen's body language, vocal tone, and breathing rate.

Related Chapters

- Boost Your Teen's Self-Esteem
- Make Your Teen Feel Valued
- Say "I Love You"
- Tackle Tough Topics
- Breakups and Broken Hearts
- Bullying
- Cutting and Self-Harm
- Depression
- Divorce
- Death and Dying
- Stress/Pressure to Succeed
- Suicide and Suicidal Thoughts
- Toxic Relationships and Abuse

9 Power Phrases to Confront a Teen Who's Lying

"No legacy is so rich as honesty."—William Shakespeare

1. Can you please explain why you feel the need to lie to me? How can I make you feel more comfortable about being honest with me?
2. Help me understand why you thought lying was the best choice in this situation? Is there a more responsible approach that you could have taken?
3. How could your lie have hurt someone?
4. How do you feel when you are lied to?
5. I am responsible for keeping you safe. I can't do that if I don't have all the information. When you lie to me and give me false information, I no longer have confidence that you'll be OK on your own.
6. I heard that you <insert behavior>. I'd like to hear your side of the story. I trust you to tell me the truth this time.
7. I want to understand why you chose to lie about <situation>. I promise not to freak out if you tell me what happened. At the same time, you have to learn to accept the consequences of what you did.
8. Instead of lying to me about <situation>, I'd rather you tell me the truth, and we can work together to find a solution that doesn't break the house rules.
9. Why do you think I am upset that you lied to me?

Did You Know?

Teens lie to:

1. Avoid disappointing you.
2. Do things you wouldn't allow.
3. Dodge punishment or unpleasant tasks.
4. Escape embarrassment.
5. Feel in control.

6. Impress peers.
7. Protect you.
8. Test limits.

Talking Tip

Studies show that over 90 percent of teens lie to their parents.[4] So don't freak out if your teen is one of them—and don't assume your teen is not.

Related Tools

- Lying-Tells Cheat Sheet

Related Chapters

- Address Your Teen's Disrespect
- Challenge a Sense of Entitlement
- Clarify the Facts
- Coax Your Teen to Open Up to You
- Encourage Accountability
- Tackle Tough Topics

12 Power Phrases to Cool Down a Heated Situation

"Anger and intolerance are the enemies of correct understanding." —Gandhi

1. I am so upset right now I can't talk nicely, so I am going to <calming technique> until I calm down.
2. I feel like you can't hear what I have to say when you're so <emotion>. Then I get frustrated. I'd like to talk about this later when we're both able to listen.
3. I understand that you want <request>, but <undesirable behavior> is not the way to go about it. I'm happy to listen to your request when you're ready to talk respectfully.
4. I'd like to discuss this more when we are both calm before making a decision. Let's take a breather and regroup at <time/date>.
5. I'll be glad to listen to you when your voice is as low as mine. Take your time.
6. It's OK to feel <emotion>, but it's not OK to <undesirable behavior> when you do. What helps me when I'm <emotion> is to <go for a brisk walk/write in your journal/talk about how you feel/etc.>.
7. This conversation isn't going productively. Let's try again at <time/date>.
8. We seem to be working against each other rather than together. What can I do to help change that?
9. What are you trying to achieve by <undesirable behavior>? Is there a more effective way to express yourself?
10. What are you trying to tell me with your <emotional behavior>?
11. You seem very <emotion> right now. That's OK, but I can't help you when you're so emotional. Let's take a break and talk about this at <time/date>.
12. You're clearly <emotion>. What's that all about?

Did You Know?

Studies show that teens who were consistently yelled at or criticized by their parents were more likely to do the very things their parents were trying to stop: lying, cheating, stealing, and fighting.[5] Additionally, reacting in anger (e.g., yelling, threatening, criticizing, etc.) …

- causes more anger.
- discourages your teen from coming to you in the future.
- inhibits problem-solving.
- models poor communication skills.
- sparks teen rebellion.
- turns interactions into power struggles.
- undermines parental authority.

Talking Tip

Stay calm, cool, and collected.

Parents often get frustrated with their teens and attempt to gain control of the situation through anger: yelling, threatening, physical punishment, sarcasm, etc.. However, your anger simply sparks more anger in your teen and eventually the negative emotion will spiral out of control. By staying calm instead, you're not only creating an opportunity to resolve the situation more effectively and quickly, you're also showing your teen that you are in control of both the situation *and* your emotions. Eventually your teen will learn that anger gets him nowhere and will start to imitate your emotional control.

Quick Trick

6 Hot Tips for Keeping Your Cool

1. Breathe, tense, release.
2. Roll your shoulders.

3. Squeeze something squishy.
4. Suck on a sweet or chew gum.
5. Talk slow and low.
6. Smile.

Related Tools

- Behavior Agreement

Related Chapters

- Address Your Teen's Disrespect
- Buy More Time to Respond
- Challenge a Sense of Entitlement
- Confront a Teen Who's Lying
- Enforce Rules and Consequences
- Respond to Arguing
- Control Extreme Emotions

18 Power Phrases to Encourage Accountability

(Learning from Mistakes)

"Accountability breeds response-ability." —Stephen R. Covey

1. As long as I know where you are, who you're with, and when you'll return, I can continue to trust you with more freedom. I appreciate your understanding and cooperation with this.
2. Every mistake gives us an opportunity to learn. Tell me one mistake you made today and what you learned from it.
3. Everyone has the right to make mistakes. I love you too much to keep trying to fix things for you. From now on I'm going to try to back off and give you the space you need to make your own choices and learn from your own mistakes. How does that sound?
4. How can you handle a similar situation in the future to get a better outcome?
5. I feel a bit let down that you didn't take this task seriously and put more effort into it. When do you think you can complete this correctly?
6. I feel sad when I see you missing an opportunity to learn and grow. Can you think of a way to do this that would help you get more out of it?
7. I understand you're upset with <insert name of person>, but the only person you can change is yourself. Let's focus on what *you* can do to fix this.
8. If something like this happens again, what can you do to get the results you want?
9. It looks like you have a problem to solve. I'm here if you want to bounce some ideas off of me.
10. It sounds like you are blaming <person/situation> for your <behavior>, but the only person responsible for your actions is *you*. How could you have handled this situation differently?

11. It's OK to make mistakes. It means that you're thinking, making decisions, and taking risks.
12. Mistakes are inevitable and acceptable. Why do you feel the need to hide this from me?
13. What are you going to do?
14. What could you have done to prevent this from happening? How can you do that next time?
15. What do you think will happen next if you do that?
16. What was your role in this?
17. When you make a mistake, I'd like to hear about it. Then we can talk about what you learned and what you can do in the future to keep from making that mistake again.
18. You're right. The situation stinks. What can you do to make it better?

Did You Know?

Shame and fear drive us to cover up, deny, and blame others for our mistakes. Even Koko, the gorilla famous for learning sign language, once blamed her pet kitten for pulling a sink out of the wall.

Talking Tip

Mistakes are going to happen. When they do, there is no need to dwell on them and dredge up the shame and embarrassment that goes along with it. If your teen recognizes his mistake, chances are he won't repeat it on his own volition. Focus instead on the lesson and what you both can learn from the mistake.

Quick Trick

How to create a culture of accountability in your home:

- Accept your teen's apologies.
- Applaud rather than punish honesty.

- Create a "blame-free" zone.
- Give your teen a chance to fix her mistakes.
- Own up to your own mistakes to show your teen how it's done.

Related Tools

- Curfew Agreement
- Dating Agreement
- Homework Agreement
- Household Responsibilities Agreement

Related Chapters

- Challenge a Sense of Entitlement
- Clarify the Facts (Reflective Listening)
- Confront a Teen Who's Lying
- Prompt Your Teen to Problem-Solve
- Spark Collaboration
- Bullying
- Cheating in School
- Sex: Birth Control
- Shoplifting/Stealing
- Technology Use and Safety
- Underachievement

20 Power Phrases to Enforce Rules and Consequences

(Effective Discipline)

"The fewer rules a coach has, the fewer rules there are for players to break." —John Madden

1. Are you aware of how your <insert behavior> affects ...?
2. Because you made the choice to <action>, you also chose to accept the consequence, which is ...
3. Even though you've received fair warning, I see that you still chose to <behavior>. As you know, the consequence for that is ...
4. Explain to me why you decided to break our rule that ...
5. First, I'm interested in the facts. Once we've established the facts, I'm open to hearing why you ... Then we can determine the best way to handle it.
6. I expect that when you say you're going to <behavior>, that you'll be good to your word.
7. I understand that you're feeling <emotion> about some things and I'm sorry for the role I've played in that, but it doesn't excuse you for <behavior>. I want to work with you to resolve our issues so that you can feel better, stay safe, and our family can be stronger. Are you willing to make some changes along with the rest of us so that we can resolve these problems?
8. I would like to discuss <behavior> and focus on how to improve it. I also must remind you of the consequences if it continues.
9. Is there any confusion about what the rules about <behavior> are?
10. Please consider this your first verbal warning. As you know, the consequence for <behavior> is ...
11. Something is making it difficult for you to follow our rule that ... Can you tell me what that is?
12. The rule that <rule> is designed to <purpose> and I will enforce it. You know the consequence for breaking this rule is ...

13. We agreed that you would <action> by <time>. I expect you to follow that rule. How can we make sure that will happen?
14. What do you believe the rule is? Do you think that rule is important and necessary? Why or why not?
15. What time can we expect you to be home? If you're not going to make it by then, will you call by <time> to let me know?
16. When I expect you to <behavior> and you don't, I worry.
17. When you <behavior>, it breaks our rule that <rule>. We agreed the consequence for breaking that rule is ...
18. Why do you continue to <behavior>? I thought we agreed that the rule for that is ...
19. You know how I feel about this, but ultimately it's your decision. Would you rather <behavior> or <consequence>?
20. You know our rule regarding <behavior> is <rule>. You didn't follow that rule. As we discussed, the consequence for that is ...

Did You Know?

The prefrontal cortex, the portion of the brain that discerns between good and bad choices, is still developing during adolescence. This means teens aren't always capable of realizing the consequences of their actions. This is why setting clear rules and guidelines for them is essential. It also means that making your teen feel bad about a poor decision is counterproductive. It won't help her make better choices in the future, but it could shake her self-confidence.

Talking Tip

Sit down with your teen when you're both calm and work together to define your house rules and the consequences for breaking those rules. Then, when your teen breaks a rule, instead of resorting to yelling and power struggles, all you need to do is enforce the consequence matter-of-factly and move on.

Related Tools

- Behavior Agreement
- Cell Phone Agreement
- Curfew Agreement
- Dating Agreement
- Driving Agreement
- Homework Agreement
- Household Responsibilities Agreement

Related Chapters

- Buy More Time to Respond
- Challenge a Sense of Entitlement
- Clarify the Facts
- Cool Down a Heated Situation
- Encourage Accountability
- Give Constructive Feedback
- Grab (and Keep) Your Teen's Attention
- Persuade Your Teen to Do Something
- Prevent Misunderstandings
- Respond to Arguing
- Say "No" with Authority
- Spark Collaboration

11 Power Phrases to Give Constructive Feedback

"We all need people who will give us feedback. That's how we improve." —Bill Gates

1. I am generally pleased with how you <insert task>, especially <provide good example>. There is one thing you may want to work on though ...
2. I appreciate your effort, but <problem>. Have you considered trying ...?
3. I do understand what you're saying, I just disagree with it and I believe it's in your best interest if . . .
4. I know you work really hard at <task>, and I appreciate that. But I've noticed that <problem>. I used to do this when I was about your age, too. May I show you the way I've learned how to do it?
5. I like that you took on <task>. I have an idea that might make it even easier for you if you're interested.
6. What obstacles are you experiencing and what can I do now and in the future to help you overcome them?
7. What you just did is unacceptable because <problem>. What can you do differently in the future?
8. When you said <quote>, I felt <emotion>. Is there another way you can express yourself that won't come across so hurtful?
9. You are expected to <task>, but what is happening instead is <problem>. What can you do differently?
10. You are usually <quality>, but lately this is slipping. What's going on?
11. You know you shouldn't have <behavior>. Let's talk about how you can handle the situation better next time.

Did You Know?

Praise may actually have a reverse impact on teens. Vague compliments, such as "good job" or "you're smart," often come across as condescending or empty and meaningless rather than supportive. Constructive feedback (both negative and positive) has more weight because it is well thought out and provides specific guidance for improvement.[6]

Talking Tip

To give constructive feedback the R.I.G.H.T way, keep it:

- **R**espectful. Make sure the person is open to getting feedback.
- **I**ssue-specific. Focus on a specific skill or behavior.
- **G**oal-focused. Focus on how to achieve the desired outcome.
- **H**elpful. Offer suggestions for performing a skill more effectively.
- **T**imely. Provide feedback within a reasonable time frame.

Related Chapters

- Boost Your Teen's Self-Esteem
- Challenge a Sense of Entitlement
- Encourage Accountability
- Grab (and Keep) Your Teen's Attention
- Make Your Teen Feel Valued
- Motivate Your Teen
- Persuade Your Teen to Do Something
- Prevent Misunderstandings
- Prompt Your Teen to Problem-Solve

9 Power Phrases to Grab (and Keep) Your Teen's Attention

"A good teacher, like a good entertainer, first must hold his audience's attention, then he can teach his lesson." —John Henrik Clarke

1. Here's what matters most about this ...
2. If you remember one thing, remember this ...
3. Listen carefully to what I'm about to say ...
4. The key point is ...
5. The one thing you don't want to forget is ...
6. This is important ...
7. This is the best part ...
8. This next point is critical ...
9. You'll appreciate this ...

Did You Know?

Our average attention span is only 8 to 9 seconds—so keep it short and simple![7]

Talking Tip

7 tricks to hold your teen's attention:

1. Alert your teen that he needs to listen by using the phrases above.
2. Ask open-ended questions to get her involved.
3. Keep it short and to the point.
4. Make it relatable to him.
5. Reduce outside distractions—turn off all electronics.
6. Tell a story (make it funny if possible).
7. Use props and gestures to support what you're saying.

Related Chapters

- Cool Down a Heated Situation

14 Power Phrases to Make Your Teen Feel Valued

"I consider my ability to arouse enthusiasm among men the greatest asset I possess. The way to develop the best that is in a man is by appreciation and encouragement."—Charles Schwab

1. I appreciate that you …
2. I couldn't have done this without you. Thank you!
3. I know you don't like doing this, and I thank you for doing it anyway. It helps so much.
4. I love that I can count on you to …
5. I want to thank you for ...
6. I was pleased to see you ...
7. It was so thoughtful of you to …
8. Thanks for helping. That made a big difference.
9. We make a great team.
10. What a great idea.
11. Wow! You've been a huge help with ...
12. You made my day by …
13. You said that you would <task> and you did. Thank you!
14. You're a lifesaver for …

Did You Know?

A happiness study found that teens remember 81 percent of negative words and only 31 percent of positive words. Yet, to be really happy, they need to experience at least three positive emotions to every negative one. How can you help tip the scale in your teen's favor?[8]

Talking Tip

Parents often complain that teens today have no manners. If you don't want your teen to be labeled as rude, the most powerful thing you can do is model the polite behaviors you want her to embrace. For example, the more you say, "please," "thank you," and "you're welcome," to your teen, the better the odds that she'll say them back to you (without even having to nag).

Related Chapters

- Boost Your Teen's Self-Esteem
- Say "I Love You"
- Spark Collaboration

27 Power Phrases to Motivate Your Teen

"Our greatest weakness lies in giving up. The most certain way to succeed is always to try just one more time." —Thomas Edison

1. All I ask is that you make an effort.
2. Clearly you're pretty worried about <insert task>. I want to see you succeed. What can I do to support you or relieve some of your stress—besides doing <task> for you, of course.
3. How can I best help you stay on track?
4. I can see you're frustrated with <task>, but I also can see how much you've improved already. Keep at it, and before you know it, it'll seem much easier.
5. I can tell you've put a lot of effort into this already, it shows. Let's work together some more and figure out the rest.
6. I have no problem with you disliking <task>. But I do have a problem with you quitting. Can you think of a way to make it more enjoyable?
7. I know you don't really like <subject/task>, but it is one of those things that you have to do so that you can do what you want to do, like ... It may stink now, but when you finally reach your goal, you'll be so happy you did it!
8. I know you have to do <project/task> and you're stressed-out about it. One thing that works for me is taking an occasional break. For example, you could work on it for 45 minutes, then take a 10 to 15 minute break to chill before getting back to it for another 45 minutes. Want to try it for a while and see if it works?
9. I'm impressed that you took on such a challenging project. It's going to take a lot of work, but wow, you're going to learn a lot of amazing things.
10. If you keep chipping away at <task> one step at a time, you'll be done before you know it.

11. If you put in your best effort every time, I promise you, you may be outscored from time to time, but you will never lose.
12. You may have too many things on your plate right now. Let's take a few minutes to write down all the things that you have to do, then prioritize them. Maybe there are some things that we can cut from your schedule, so you don't feel so stressed.
13. Let's talk to someone who is doing what you want to do and find out what she had to do to be successful. Maybe she'll have some tips for you too.
14. Make it happen. I believe in you.
15. Remember your goal to <describe teen's goal>? Completing <task> will get you closer to achieving that.
16. Sometimes the fear of failure makes it really difficult for me to start something. What makes it difficult for you to try something?
17. That does seem like a big task. If we break it down into smaller steps, it won't seem so overwhelming. Would you like me to help you do that?
18. The things that are worth the most are often the most difficult to obtain—otherwise everyone would <do/have> it. Once you reach your goal, you're going to be so happy that you didn't give up.
19. This is going to be a tough task, and I'll be here to help you any way I can. I simply want to thank you for taking on this challenge.
20. Try to stay focused on <the task> for the next 20 minutes and then take a 10-minute break. Keep doing that until you're done. Let me know how it goes.
21. We'll work it out if it doesn't go right, but I think you can do it. Just try.
22. What is the consequence if you don't do <task>? Is it worth it?
23. Why are you having a hard time with <task>? How can we make it more manageable for you?
24. Why are you so committed to <something they love>? How could you take some of the ambition you have for that and transfer it to your schoolwork, which is also important? Could you figure out

a way to make your homework more fun and maybe even involve your friends?

25. You have <number> things you have to do this week, right? Let's write them down along with the amount of time you think it'll take to complete them. Now, let's look at your schedule for the week and see where we can fit these in. Does that sound good?
26. You need to focus on becoming just a little bit better every day. Then, one day in the near future, you'll suddenly realize that you're a lot better than you were when you started.
27. You've made great progress so far and it should all be downhill from here.

Did You Know?

Teens have an underactive ventral striatal circuit, which is part of the brain involved in motivation. The teen brain is also very susceptible to stress. Add to that the fact that teens need more sleep than adults, but often get less, and are in a constant state of sleep deprivation, and it's no wonder that teens struggle to get motivated and are inclined to steer clear of stressful situations. Instead of reacting in anger to your teen's perceived disrespect, try empathy to encourage him to get off the couch.

Talking Tip

6 Teen Motivators

1. Appreciation: They'll do better if they feel better.
2. Encouragement and support: Let your teen know you believe in her.
3. Fun: Make the task into a game or a challenge
4. Humor: Lighten the load by lightening things up.
5. Involvement: Invite your teen to participate in problem-solving.
6. Natural consequences: Allow your teen to fail and feel the discomfort of the consequences.

Related Chapters

- Challenge a Sense of Entitlement
- Encourage Accountability
- Make Your Teen Feel Valued
- Persuade Your Teen to Do Something
- Prompt Your Teen to Problem-Solve
- Spark Collaboration

24 Power Phrases to Persuade Your Teen to Do Something

"Persuasion is often more effectual than force."—Aesop

1. As soon as you've completed <insert task>, you can get right back to ...
2. Could you, please <task>? Thank you so much!
3. Feel free to <request> as soon as <task> is done.
4. I am aware of how busy you are, however I'd appreciate it if you could spare a moment to help me with ...
5. I can't tell you how much I'd appreciate it if you would ...
6. I could really use your help with ...
7. I hate getting into an argument every time I ask you to <task>. But I really depend on you to get it done. How can we make sure it gets accomplished without making you feel like I'm nagging you?
8. I have two tasks that need to be completed by <time/date>: <task 1> and <task 2>. I'll let you pick which one you want to do and I'll take the other.
9. I have a job that has your name on it because you've got a knack for ...
10. I know you'd rather be <activity>, but I need <task> done by <time>. The sooner you finish, the sooner you'll be free to do what you want.
11. I need <task> completed by <time/date> because <reason>. Can I depend on you?
12. I would be so grateful if you could ...
13. I'll be happy to <request> as soon as you've completed <task>.
14. I'm asking you to <task> because I know I can count on you.
15. I've been thinking. I push you to do <task> <when/how> I think is best. But moving forward, I'm going to trust you to do <task> <when/how> is right for you. All I ask is that it's done sometime before <time/date> because ...
16. Is there any reason that you wouldn't be able to get this done by <time/date>?

17. It is very important to me that you <behavior> so that I know you're OK.
18. It would mean a lot to me if you would ...
19. Thanks ahead of time. I really appreciate it.
20. What do you need from me to be able to complete <task> by <time/date>?
21. Would you be willing to ...?
22. Would you rather <option 1> or <option 2>?
23. You don't want to <task>? No problem. So I guess that means you'd prefer to <consequence> instead?
24. You may <option 1> or <option 2>. It's your choice.

Did You Know?

Pride is a huge motivator. If your teen feels good about his contribution and is recognized and appreciated for it, he'll almost always be more willing to help out when asked.

Talking Tip

3 A's of Persuasion

1. **A**cknowledgement: Look your teen in the eye and acknowledge that you need her help.
2. **A**sking nicely**:** Instead of making a demand, ask your teen nicely. He'll be much more willing to help if he thinks he has a choice.
3. **A**ppreciation: Let your teen know how much you value her help. Often a simple "thank you" will do.

Related Tools

- Behavior Agreement
- Curfew Agreement
- Homework Agreement
- Household Responsibilities Agreement

Related Chapters

- Challenge a Sense of Entitlement
- Encourage Accountability
- Enforce Rules and Consequences
- Give Constructive Feedback
- Make Your Teen Feel Valued
- Motivate Your Teen
- Prompt Your Teen to Problem-Solve
- Spark Collaboration

20 Power Phrases to Prevent Misunderstandings

"It is not enough for parents to understand children. They must accord children the privilege of understanding them." —Milton Sapirstein

1. Am I making sense?
2. Apparently I wasn't clear. Let me say it another way.
3. Does that answer your question?
4. I can see why you thought that's what I said, but it's not. What I intended to say was ...
5. I don't understand what you mean. Could you give me an example?
6. I get the impression that <insert observation>. Is that correct?
7. I may not understand you correctly, and I find myself taking what you said personally. What I thought you just said is … Is that what you meant?
8. I think I see where you're coming from. You're saying that … Is that right?
9. I want to make sure I was clear. What did you hear me say?
10. I'd like to understand why you think that.
11. I'll give you an example of what I mean.
12. I'm getting the impression that <observation>. Am I close?
13. I'm listening, but I don't understand. What do you mean by ...?
14. I'm not explaining myself clearly. Let me try it a different way.
15. Is there anything else you would like to know about …?
16. So what you're saying is <paraphrase>. Yes?
17. That's not what I meant. Let me try again.
18. What did I leave out?
19. What I thought you said is <paraphrase>. Is that what you meant?
20. What questions do you have?

Did You Know?

When your teen misunderstands you it may be frustrating, but it's not necessarily her fault. Because the adolescent brain is still under construction, your teen organizes and understands information differently than you do. This means that you can never assume that what you say to your teen is what your teen actually hears.

Talking Tip

7 Musts for a Clear Message

1. Be *very* specific.
2. Get to the point.
3. Keep it brief.
4. Provide examples.
5. Repeat and rephrase.
6. Say what you *do* want instead of what you don't.
7. Use simple words.

Related Tools

- Behavior Agreement
- Cell Phone Agreement
- Curfew Agreement
- Dating Agreement
- Driving Agreement
- Homework Agreement
- Household Responsibilities Agreement

Related Chapters

- Clarify the Facts
- Coax Your Teen to Open Up to You
- Enforce Rules and Consequences

27 Power Phrases to Prompt Your Teen to Problem-Solve

"Tell me and I forget, teach me and I may remember, involve me and I learn."—Benjamin Franklin

1. <Skill> is a skill you need to master and <task> will help you improve that skill.
2. Good luck! I believe in you.
3. How are you going to handle it when …?
4. I asked you to <insert task> because I believe you will be good at it. I'm leaving it up to you to figure it out.
5. I'll help you if you get stuck, but I won't do it for you. I believe you can do <task>. Give it another try.
6. I'm guessing that didn't go as planned. What went wrong? How can you fix it? OK, try again.
7. If it's that important to you, I am confident that you will find a way to achieve it.
8. Is that a good choice for you?
9. Let's weigh the alternatives and decide which is best.
10. On a scale from 1 to 10, how confident are you that you can …? Why a <number>? What would it take to bring it up to a <higher number>?
11. That's a good question, what do you think?
12. There is more than one way to solve a problem. What options do you see?
13. What are some other ways you could have handled the situation?
14. What are your next steps?
15. What are some of your options?
16. What do you think caused the problem?
17. What do you think went wrong? Is there something that you can do differently the next time?
18. What do you think will happen next if you do that?
19. What do you think you should do?
20. What have you tried so far? What haven't you tried yet?

21. What worked before?
22. What would you like to see happen? How can you achieve that?
23. What would you prefer instead of this?
24. Where can you get the information you need?
25. Which approach would work best for you?
26. Why do you think this happened?
27. You're resourceful. If you want that, I'm sure you can find an acceptable way to get it.

Did You Know?

The more you stress over a problem that your teen owns, the less he'll take ownership of it and the more likely the problem will get bigger. Take the opportunity to teach your teen the essential skill of problem-solving, but don't solve it for him.

Talking Tip

Teach your teen the 7 steps to problem solving:

1. Define the problem.
2. Identify the ideal outcome.
3. Break it down into manageable pieces.
4. Brainstorm 4 or more possible solutions.
5. Pick the best solution.
6. Take action.
7. Evaluate the results.

Related Chapters

- Buy More Time to Respond
- Challenge a Sense of Entitlement
- Encourage Accountability
- Give Constructive Feedback
- Spark Collaboration

11 Power Phrases to Respond to Arguing

"The aim of an argument should not be victory, but progress."—Joseph Joubert

1. I am basing my decision upon what I know, which is <paraphrase>. If you have additional information you'd like to share with me, I'll take it into consideration and let you know if it affects my final decision.
2. I can see why you see it that way, but have you considered ...?
3. I hear what you're saying, however when you <behavior> I worry that <concern>. Do you have any suggestions?
4. I respect your opinion. If you have additional points you'd like me to consider, please write them down and we can discuss them at <time>.
5. If you have a problem with my decision, I am happy to discuss it with you—calmly. Otherwise, I expect your cooperation. Is there anything you see as unreasonable about that?
6. If you were in my position, what would you do?
7. It's your choice. You can decide to <behavior> OR deal with the consequence, which is ...
8. Up to a point I agree with you. What I question is <concern>.
9. What evidence do you have for that claim?
10. Yes, I guess that's an option. Why do you think it's the best one?
11. Your opinion is important to me, and I'd like to get your input before I make my decision, however it is *my* decision to make.

Did You Know?

"We tell parents to think of those arguments not as nuisance but as a critical training ground."—Joseph P. Allen, Psychologist

Talking Tip

How to win an argument:

1. Remain calm and respectful. (Attack the issue, not the person.)
2. State your opinion clearly and calmly.
3. Provide 1 to 3 logical reasons why you hold that opinion.
4. Back your reasons up with evidence and examples.
5. Listen to counter-arguments and acknowledge them.
6. Ask probing questions to either uncover flaws in an argument or to understand it better.
7. Respond with a rebuttal. (Point out fallacies, flawed reasoning, lack of evidence, etc.)
8. Be willing to compromise or concede. It's about determining *what* is right, not *being* right.

Related Chapters

- Address Your Teen's Disrespect
- Buy More Time to Respond
- Cool Down a Heated Situation
- Encourage Accountability
- Enforce Rules and Consequences
- Prevent Misunderstandings
- Say "No" with Authority

20 Power Phrases to Say "I Love You"

(Without Totally Embarrassing Your Teen)

"Too often we underestimate the power of a touch, a smile, a kind word, a listening ear, an honest compliment, or the smallest act of caring, all of which have the potential to turn a life around." —Leo Buscaglia

1. I always have time for you.
2. I am thankful for you because ...
3. I believe in you.
4. I enjoy spending time with you.
5. I love you.
6. I trust you.
7. I'm glad you called.
8. I'm listening.
9. I'm so happy you're my child.
10. I've got your back.
11. It's so cool that you <behavior>.
12. It's so fun to talk to you.
13. Know I'm here cheering you on.
14. There is no one I'd rather be doing this with.
15. You can talk to me anytime about anything.
16. You made that so much fun.
17. You make me proud.
18. You make me smile.
19. You mean the world to me.
20. You're very important to me.

Did You Know?

Most teens are so vulnerable that they repeatedly test their parents to see if they really love them. Make sure that your teen knows without a doubt that you love her unconditionally, even when her actions make you want to pull your hair out. One way to do this is by expressing sincere affection at least once a day—without undermining it with an "if," "and," or "but."

Talking Tip

Don't be afraid to touch your teen. Appropriate physical contact conveys your unconditional love and shouldn't be stopped just because your teen has gotten older. Some moves that exude affection, but don't invade your teen's personal space, are:

- Arm squeeze
- Hug
- Pat on the back
- Smile
- Thumbs up
- Wink

Quick Trick

3 Affectionate Actions that Speak Louder than Words

1. Spending quality time with your teen
2. Surprising your teen with small gifts or notes
3. Doing something nice for your teen without being asked

Related Chapters

- Boost Your Teen's Self-Esteem
- Comfort Your Teen
- Make Your Teen Feel Valued
- Say "I'm Sorry" with Conviction

9 Power Phrases to Say "I'm Sorry" with Conviction

"Humility is the solid foundation of all virtues." —Confucius

1. I am not proud of the way I handled <situation>. I'd like to wipe the slate clean and try again.
2. I got <emotion> when <situation>, and I let that cloud my judgment. I'm ready to listen objectively now if you'll let me.
3. I realize that my <insert behavior> was inappropriate, and I can only imagine how <emotion> that made you feel. I am very sorry.
4. I regret the hurt I caused you; it is inexcusable, and it will never happen again. Is there anything I can do to make it up to you?
5. I want to apologize for <behavior>. I hope that you will forgive me.
6. I'm sorry I did that. After some more thought, I think I made a mistake. Here's what I think might be better …
7. I've never been a parent to a <child's age>-year-old before. I'm doing my best, but I'm bound to make mistakes from time to time. I'm sorry. Thanks for being patient with me.
8. Now that I've had some time to reflect, I realize I overreacted when <situation>. I'd like to sit down and try to resolve <problem> calmly this time.
9. When I'm wrong, I admit it and I realize that <behavior> was wrong. I'm truly sorry.

Did You Know?

A sincere apology is a powerful way to gain your teen's respect and rebuild her confidence and trust in you.

Talking Tip

5 Components of an Effective Apology

1. Accept responsibility.
2. Express genuine regret.
3. Offer a sincere apology.
4. Make amends.
5. Request forgiveness.

Related Chapters

- Coax Your Teen to Open Up to You
- Cool Down a Heated Situation
- Encourage Accountability
- Respond to Arguing
- Say "I Love You"

8 Power Phrases to Say "No" with Authority

"If you have ten thousand regulations you will destroy all respect for the law."—Winston Churchill

1. Based on the information I have so far, my answer is "no." Is there anything I'm missing?
2. Because I love you and want to keep you safe, I worry about <concern>, which is why I'm saying "no." Please tell me you'll honor our rule that ...
3. I have to say no because <concern>. I'd be willing to reconsider if ...
4. I know being able to <request> is important to you. As much as I'd like to say yes, I can't because ...
5. I understand what you're asking. The thing is, we have to consider <concern> as well. I have to say no unless we can find a way around that.
6. Sorry, my answer is "no." If you don't think that's fair, feel free to write a list of reasons why I should say "yes." I promise to take them into consideration, but I can't promise to change my mind.
7. That breaks our house rule that <rule>. Unless you have a good reason I should make an exception this time, the answer is "no."
8. Yes, as soon as you've completed <task>.

Did You Know?

Many parents are afraid to set limits because they think it will build a wall between them and their teen. In truth, limits actually show your teen that you care about him.

Talking Tip

To speak with authority:

- Avoid mumbling or trailing off.
- Don't yell.
- Lower your voice.
- Make eye contact.
- Slow down.
- Stand tall.
- Stay calm.
- Take time to listen too.

Related Chapters

- Address Your Teen's Disrespect
- Buy More Time to Respond
- Challenge a Sense of Entitlement
- Enforce Rules and Consequences
- Respond to Arguing

23 Power Phrases to Spark Collaboration

"The secret is to gang up on the problem, rather than each other." —Thomas Stallkamp

1. Do you see a better way of doing this?
2. How can we resolve this?
3. How do you think we can make this work?
4. How might I gain your cooperation?
5. How would you feel about …?
6. I understand what you're saying, however we also need to take <concern> into consideration. How do you think we can make this work for everyone involved?
7. I value your input.
8. I want to make sure that you have a say in this too. What is your opinion about ...?
9. I would really like your help with this.
10. I'd love your thoughts about …
11. I'm considering <solution>. What do you think?
12. In your opinion, what should we do?
13. Is there anything that you want to make sure we consider?
14. It seems like we're at a deadlock here. You want … and I want … How can we meet halfway?
15. Let's find the best way to get this done together.
16. Let's see if there are any ideas we can come up with that would give you a little more of what you want and still give me peace of mind.
17. Please tell me what you like about this idea/plan. What would make you like it more?
18. There's got to be a solution that will work for both of us. Any ideas?
19. What do you suggest?
20. What do you think about …?
21. What have I overlooked?
22. What would make this better for everyone involved?

23. Would you be OK with …?

Did You Know?

One of the best methods of reducing parent-teen conflict is collaborative problem-solving—finding a solution that satisfies both you and your teen.

Talking Tips

6 Steps to a Successful Collaboration

1. Define the WHYs: What is the purpose of the rule (e.g., keep teen safe)?
2. Share your WHATs: What does each of you want? What are your goals (e.g., have teen home at reasonable time)?
3. Brainstorm some HOWs: Come up with all possible ways to achieve your whats. This should be a judgment-free exercise.
4. Agree on *the* HOW: Pick the solution that best achieves both of your goals.
5. Plan for WHAT IFs: What are the consequences if the rule is broken?
6. Write it all down: Get it on paper to prevent disagreements later.

Related Chapters

- Boost Your Teen's Self-Esteem
- Clarify the Facts
- Encourage Accountability
- Enforce Rules and Consequences
- Make Your Teen Feel Valued
- Motivate Your Teen
- Prevent Misunderstandings

40 Power Phrases to Tackle Tough Topics

"I would rather be uncomfortable with the truth than to be lied to in comfort."—Jesse Ventura

1. Can you tell me what you already know about …?
2. Do you know anyone that has done <behavior> or wants to? Have you thought about it?
3. Do you know anyone who is …? How did the kids in school react to him?
4. Do you know what that means?
5. Even if you've already <behavior>, you can stop. You don't have to continue doing something that doesn't feel right to you.
6. Have any of your friends started …? What do you think about that?
7. Have you heard anything about <behavior> at school? What are your thoughts about it?
8. Here are the facts I know about … Is there anything else you want to know?
9. Here's what I believe about … What are your beliefs?
10. Hey, we haven't talked about <behavior> in a while. I get it; you're uncomfortable. But it's my job to make sure that you are healthy and safe. Do you have some time to talk now?
11. I don't know the answer to that. Let's see what we can find out together.
12. I don't know, but I'll find out.
13. I hope you are comfortable coming to me with your questions about <behavior>, but here are some reliable resources you can use as well.
14. I just read this article about … I'd be curious to get your take on it.
15. I know it might be scary for you to talk to me about <behavior>, but there is nothing you can say or do to cause me to stop loving you.
16. I want to make sure that you have accurate information about <behavior> so that you aren't confused or misled by kids at school.

However that doesn't mean I think it's OK for you to <behavior> right now. I hope that you'll wait until <age/milestone> because …

17. I'm glad that you came to me about …
18. I'm happy to tell you about <behavior>, but it will help me explain it better if you can tell me what you already know about it.
19. I'm wondering where you heard about … Let's make sure everything you heard is accurate.
20. I've been hearing people talk about <behavior> lately, do you know what that is? Do you have any questions about it?
21. It's so important that we keep talking like this, even if it's awkward sometimes. Just know I'm always here to listen.
22. Thanks for being honest with me about <behavior>. I think it's important to have open communication and for you to stay true to yourself when it comes to …
23. That's an importation question, and I want to make sure that I give you a good answer. Let me think about it for a while.
24. This conversation is really important, so I promise to do my best.
25. This might be a little awkward for us, but here it goes ...
26. Ultimately, the choice is yours, so I want to make sure that you have all the information you need to make the safest/smartest choice.
27. What did your friends say about <behavior>? Do you agree?
28. What do you think <behavior> is? What's your opinion about it?
29. What do you think about this situation in the news? What do your friends think about it?
30. What do you think about …?
31. What have you heard about …?
32. What questions do you have for me about …?
33. What words or terms do you hear at school or in the media that you don't fully understand? I may not know the meaning either, but we can look it up together.
34. When I don't have to worry about <behavior>, I'll let you <privilege>.
35. Why do you want to <behavior> now?
36. Wow. That's a tough question. What do you think?

37. Yes, I did <behavior> when I was younger, and here's how I feel about it.
38. You know, I'm uncomfortable talking about <behavior> because my parents never talked with me about it. But I want us to be able to talk about anything—including <behavior>—so please come to me if you have any questions. And if I don't know the answer, I'll find out.
39. You need a plan for dealing with <difficult situation> in case it arises. Let's figure out in advance what you can say and do to stand up for what you believe.
40. You're getting to an age when you're going to have lots of questions about <behavior>. I'm happy to talk to you about it any time.

Did You Know?

During adolescence, teens need to experiment and explore in order to develop a strong self-identity. You can help by making your home a safe place to express different views and ideas. If you don't agree with your teen's opinions, you can keep communication open by acknowledging and reflecting your teen's feelings without actually supporting his beliefs.

Talking Tip

Before discussing a tough topic, ask your teen what she already knows and if she has any specific questions. If she is uncomfortable talking, have her write the questions down. This will help you determine where to start and what information you need to clear up.

Related Chapters

- Appearance
- Body Image
- Breakups and Broken Hearts
- Being Bullied
- Bullying Others

17 Power Phrases about Appearance

(Clothing, Grooming, Makeup, Tattoos, Piercings, Etc.)

"In the game of parenting, it's not about the length of his hair. It's about his heart."—Dr. Michael J. Bradley

1. Are you sure that <article of clothing/style> complies with your school's dress code? What is the policy for …?
2. I know you love that <article of clothing>, but it is beyond the limits of what I think is appropriate for <school/church/etc.> because … Am I crazy?
3. I love your <top/hairstyle/color combination/etc.>, but I'm concerned about <part of look> because … Is that the message you're trying to give?
4. I think I'm a pretty reasonable parent, and I know what a great kid you are, but I'm not sure <name/place> will understand your <article of clothing/style>. Any ideas on how you can switch it up a bit this one time, out of respect for …?
5. I think it's great that you are experimenting with different looks and styles. What is it about this one that appeals to you?
6. I want to know where you plan on getting it done first. It's critical that you go to a licensed tattoo artist/parlor to lower your risk of infection, bleeding, swelling, and pain.
7. I'm all about self-expression. What are you trying to say about yourself with this look?
8. I'm sure this means a lot to you, but I can't approve of you doing this now because … However, once you turn 18, you'll no longer need my permission. Is there any reason you can't wait until then?
9. I've noticed a lot of kids dressing like that lately. I try to be open-minded, but I can't figure this one out. Why is this style so popular now?

10. If you wait until <date> and you still feel strongly about it then, I'll support you.
11. OK. As long as you're comfortable with the possible repercussions. You do know what those are, right?
12. That's a daring move. I find that sitting on a life-changing decision like that for a few weeks is a good idea. Especially when it's something so permanent.
13. That's a huge decision. Will you humor me and write out a list of pros and cons first? I just want you to be 100 percent confident that this is what you want.
14. What do you think about getting <temporary solution> first to test it out? Then you can be 100 percent sure you want it before you make it permanent. My treat.
15. What does getting this mean to you? Why is it so important to you? Why now?
16. What would it mean to not be allowed to have it?
17. Wow, that look makes a really bold statement. I wouldn't have had the courage to pull that off when I was your age.

Did You Know?

40% of teenagers have tattoos and nearly 25% have a piercing somewhere other than their earlobe.[9]

Talking Tip

Experimenting with different looks is a healthy way for teens to test out a variety of "personalities" on the road to determining their own self-identity and establishing independence. Try to give them some room to explore, unless you notice one of the following red flags:

1. Dramatic drop in hygiene and attention to general appearance
2. Getting in trouble at school/breaking dress codes
3. Jeopardizing health and well-being

Related Chapters

- Buy More Time to Respond
- Boost Your Teen's Self-Esteem
- Give Constructive Feedback
- Say "No" with Authority
- Tackle Tough Topics
- Promote a Positive Body Image
- Address Hygiene (or Lack Thereof)
- Cope with Peer Pressure

18 Power Phrases about Body Image

"As a child I never heard one woman say to me, I love my body. Not my mother, my elder sister, my best friend. No one woman has ever said, I am so proud of my body. So I make sure to say it to Mia, because a positive physical outlook has to start at an early age." —Kate Winslet

1. Believe it or not, it's often the things that we think are flaws that make us unique and beautiful to other people.
2. Do you feel OK about the way your body is growing? Why or why not?
3. Girls get a head start growing taller because they usually start changing around 8 to 13 and most boys start a few years after that. Depending on your genes, boys will eventually catch up and even grow taller than many girls.
4. How do you think being <thinner/more muscular/etc.> would make your life better? If you are serious about doing something about it, let's check it out with your doctor to make sure you do it in a healthy way.
5. I think you're beautiful/handsome just as you are. But, if there's something about yourself that you can change that will make you feel better about yourself, I'm happy to help you make a plan.
6. I understand. I've struggled with my body image as well and I'm sorry I've passed that insecurity on to you. Let's work together to be more accepting of who we are. How do you think we can do that?
7. If you looked like a supermodel, how would it make your life better? Is there a way to make the changes you want in your life with the natural beauty that you were born with?
8. If your changing body has you feeling sad or confused, healthy eating and exercise are the best ways to give you some control over how your body turns out.

9. Instead of focusing on what you don't like about yourself, let's look in the mirror together and find at least 3 things that you like about your body. Those are the things I'd love for you to focus on.
10. It is normal to feel self-conscious about your body during this time. You're going through a lot of changes and it takes time to adjust to those and feel comfortable in your own skin. If you have any concerns about how you are developing, please talk to me or someone else you trust. Chances are you're fine, but a little reassurance can't hurt.
11. It makes me sad that you aren't able to appreciate how amazing you are. For instance ...
12. It sounds like you are feeling really bad about yourself right now. I feel that way from time to time too. One thing that really helps me is to write a list of 10 things that I like about myself. Want to write a list together about what makes you so amazing?
13. It's natural to look at our friends for comparison. But it's not a good idea. Comparing ourselves with others can make us feel self-conscious because everyone develops differently and at different times.
14. Real people aren't perfect and perfect people aren't real. (They're usually airbrushed!) What is important is that you are healthy: in body, mind, and spirit.
15. What is it about your body that you don't like? Why? What/who are you comparing yourself to? Is that realistic?
16. Who are the people you admire the most? What is it about them that you admire? Was their appearance important to their success and accomplishments?
17. Who do you consider attractive? What makes them attractive? Why are those things important? Is there anything that is more important?
18. You look amazing/beautiful/handsome. I especially like how ...<that shirt brings out the color of your eyes/super cute your outfit is/the way you styled your hair/etc.>

Did You Know?

"Ideal beauties" like Marilyn Monroe (size 14) would be considered "overweight" by today's standards. Today, only 5 percent of American females actually have the "ideal" body type portrayed in advertising.[10] The impact: 77 percent of girls between the ages of 10 and 14 years old feel fat, ugly, depressed, and/or disgusting when they look at pictures of models and celebrities. They also are more afraid of weight gain than of getting cancer, experiencing nuclear war or losing their parents.[11]

Talking Tips

How to promote a positive body image:

- Be a good role model. Don't' criticize your body, your teen's body, or any body for that matter.
- Emphasize the importance of qualities other than appearance.
- Focus your family on health rather than weight.
- Get your teen involved in an activity that makes him feel empowered, such as sports and volunteering.
- Myth-bust the perfect body.
- Point out traits that make her attractive.

Related Chapters

- Boost Your Teen's Self-Esteem
- Comfort Your Teen
- Tackle Tough Topics
- Appearance
- Eating Disorders
- Hygiene (or Lack Thereof)
- Obesity and Weight
- Puberty (Boys)
- Puberty (Girls)

10 Power Phrases about Breakups and Broken Hearts

"Things don't go wrong and break your heart so you can become bitter and give up. They happen to break you down and build you up so you can be all that you were intended to be."—Charles Jones

1. Breakups can be really painful. It's OK to cry. It might actually make you feel better. If you want a shoulder to lean on, I'm here.
2. Getting over your ex is virtually impossible if you're still hoping you'll get back together. It's important to learn how to be happy by yourself.
3. I know it's tough, but try not to obsess about what you could have done differently. Most breakups happen just because the relationship has run its course, not because you did something wrong. Take from it what you can—things you've learned, experiences you've had, and how you can improve your next relationship.
4. I know this won't ease the pain now, but I want you to know that you're an incredible person and deserve to be with someone that appreciates you. I'm here to listen whenever you're ready to talk.
5. It can be so confusing when you really care about someone and they reject you. What do you think happened?
6. Oh honey, I'm so sorry. Do you want to tell me about it?
7. One of the most important things to do after a breakup is to deal with the sadness, pain, anger, confusion, and any other feelings that you are going through. Take as much time and space as you need to heal, and know I'm always hear if you want to talk or need a shoulder to cry on.
8. One of the worst parts of a breakup is feeling lonely and sad. In the past, you probably called your ex to make you feel better. Use all the willpower you've got to resist calling her/him and call one of your friends or come talk to me instead.
9. Why do you want to break up with her/him? What's the kindest way you can do it? How do you think s/he will react? Are you prepared for that?

10. You must be heartbroken right now and it may take a while for that pain to go away. That's OK. Let me know if you want to talk about it.

Did You Know?

Teenage girls tend to turn their emotions inward, and suffer from feelings of worthlessness and rejection. Teenage boys are more likely to react with anger and frustration.

Talking Tip

How to help mend a broken heart:

1. Just listen. Avoid advice, lectures, judgment, bashing the ex, etc.
2. Love on your teen. More than ever he needs to feel loveable.
3. Respect your teen's need for time and space.
4. Try to distract your teen with something fun.
5. Validate your teen's feelings, even if you don't understand them.

Related Chapters

- Boost Your Teen's Self-Esteem
- Comfort Your Teen
- Say "I Love You"
- Tackle Tough Topics
- Dating
- Toxic Relationships and Abuse

26 Power Phrases about Being Bullied

"No one can make you feel inferior without your consent." —Eleanor Roosevelt

1. Are there any mean kids at your school? Why do you think they're so cruel? Have you interacted with them? What happened?
2. Bullies love getting a reaction out of you. If you walk away, ignore them, or calmly and assertively tell them you're not interested in what they have to say, you're demonstrating that they don't have control over you. What do you think you can do the next time someone picks on you?
3. Bullies want to get an emotional reaction out of you. If you're in a situation where you have to deal with a bully and you can't walk away with poise, use humor—it can throw the bully off-guard. What's something you can say?
4. Despite what <bully's name> says, there are many wonderful things about you such as ... Keep those in mind instead of the messages you hear from bullies like <bully's name>.
5. Do a lot of kids get picked on at your school? Why do you think people pick on them? Has anyone ever picked on you?
6. Do you feel safe at school?
7. Do you know anyone in your school or in our neighborhood that is mean to other kids? Is there anything you can do about it?
8. Do you know anyone that uses the Internet, instant messenger, and/or email to embarrass, threaten, or scare others?
9. Do you think he is bothering you because he's having problems at home or school and making you feel bad may make him feel better?
10. Does it seem like some of your classmates don't like you? Why do you think that is?
11. Has anyone you know posted anything bad about a friend or you online? What happened afterwards?

12. I can't believe some of the cruel things people write on social media. That must be devastating to the person they bad-mouth. Has anyone ever written anything like that about you?
13. I'm glad you told me this is happening. I'm sorry you got hurt. I'm going to help you with this, and we will figure something out. You're strong and smart, and I believe in you. You're going to be able to deal with this so that it doesn't keep on happening to you. I'll stick with you until the problem is solved.
14. I'm so sorry this is happening and I'm really glad you told me. Teasing is not fair and is wrong. It really can hurt your feelings.
15. I'm so sorry your classmates have been teasing you. How does that make you feel?
16. Is someone being mean to you?
17. It is not your fault. No matter what someone says or does, you should not be ashamed of who you are or what you feel.
18. Most bullies have serious problems that have nothing to do with you. They just take every opportunity they can find to pick on others and unfortunately you ended up in the line of fire.
19. Nothing that you have done and nothing that you are has caused you to be bullied. Many bullies have low self-esteem and picking on people makes them feel more powerful. Thousands of kids who are perfectly nice get bullied every single day.
20. Realize that the people bullying you probably have problems of their own. These people are usually the types who take out their anger on other people.
21. The bully is probably unhappy and wants to make you or someone else feel as miserable as he does. Why do you think he's so unhappy?
22. There are a lot of reasons why people bully. Some are bullied themselves, at home or elsewhere; others bully when they feel stressed or overwhelmed. Why do you think <name> is picking on people? Is there something you can do to help her?
23. What can you do if someone bullies you? How can you protect yourself? Is there an authority figure you can tell?

24. What do you think you can say next time someone bullies you? What do you think might work?
25. What's going to make you feel better about this situation?
26. You are an amazing person and do not deserve to be treated like that.

Did You Know?

Your teen may be getting bullied if he is:

- Avoiding restrooms at school or any place he's alone.
- Evasive when you ask about his day in school.
- More withdrawn than usual.
- No longer associating with his regular group of friends.
- Showing marks, cuts, or bruising that lack an explanation.

Talking Tip

How to handle a bully:

1. Don't fight back!
2. Stand tall and look the bully in the eye.
3. Calmly tell the bully to stop.
4. Walk away.
5. Tell an adult.
6. Don't blame yourself.
7. Avoid places the bully hangs out or stay with friends.
8. Make new friends and get involved in activities.

Related Tools

- Reliable Resources Cheat Sheet
- Cell Phone Agreement
- Internet Use Agreement

Related Chapters

- Boost Your Teen's Self-Esteem
- Comfort Your Teen
- Tackle Tough Topics
- Bullying Others
- Popularity
- Shyness/Insecurity
- Tolerance

14 Power Phrases about Bullying Others

"What if the kid you bullied at school, grew up, and turned out to be the only surgeon who could save your life?" —Lynette Mather

1. All of us have to deal with a lot of difficult situations and emotions and we want to find ways to escape our bad feelings. But that's no excuse for making someone else feel bad. What else can you do to deal with your anger.
2. Do a lot of kids get picked on in your school? What do they get picked on for? Have you ever picked on someone? Why?
3. Do you really want people to think of you as unkind, abusive, and mean?
4. For some reason there are people who believe that you're responsible for some mean things that have been written about <name of victim>. Why do you think they would think that?
5. Having a close group of friends, or clique, is not bad. But, leaving out others from your group on purpose is considered bullying. Is there anything you can do to include these people?
6. How do you think <person> feels when you pick on him? Doesn't that bother you? How would you feel if the roles were reversed and you were the one being picked on?
7. How does it make you feel when you pick on people? Are there other ways you can take out your anger or stress?
8. I know being a teen can be really tough, but it isn't an excuse to treat people like that. They're struggling too.
9. I know deep down you are a kind person. It makes me sad to hear that people think you are mean. How does it make you feel to know people think badly of you?
10. I know you're a good person and don't want to hurt anyone; you just want to connect with them. Picking on someone is a definite way of connecting, but it doesn't work well at all—for you or for the person

you're picking on. I'd like to help you learn more positive ways to interact with people.

11. I'd like to help you learn how to manage your anger and aggression in a way that doesn't hurt anyone. Can you think of ways to do that?
12. I've heard about some really mean things some students have been saying about their peers on <social media>. I can't imagine how hurtful that can be. What are your thoughts about it? Have you experienced anything similar?
13. Remember, it's OK if you don't like everyone you meet. But it is important to be nice to everyone you meet. Why do you feel the need to be mean to people?
14. What are you trying to accomplish by picking on people? Does it work? Is there any other way to get that result that doesn't hurt other people?

Did You Know?

Name-calling is the most prevalent type of bullying, followed by teasing, rumor-spreading, physical incidents, purposeful isolation, threats, belongings being stolen, and sexual harassment. Cyber-bullying occurs with the least frequency.[12]

Talking Tip

Teens bully other teens because:

- It makes them feel powerful.
- They want attention.
- They feel pressured by their peers.
- They are prejudiced against that person.
- They have underdeveloped social skills.
- They want to gain social status/popularity.
- They want to get back at someone.

Related Tools

- Reliable Resources Cheat Sheet
- Behavior Agreement
- Cell Phone Agreement
- Internet Use Agreement

Related Chapters

- Boost Your Teen's Self-Esteem
- Challenge a Sense of Entitlement
- Coax Your Teen to Open Up to You
- Encourage Accountability
- Tackle Tough Topics
- Being Bullied
- Extreme Emotions
- Peer Pressure
- Popularity
- School Violence
- Tolerance

18 Power Phrases about Cheating in School

"I would prefer even to fail with honor than win by cheating."—Sophocles

1. Cheating may make things feel easier now, but it's going to catch up with you and make your life much tougher when you're older.
2. Do you feel like this class/subject is too difficult for you?
3. Do you understand what's considered cheating?
4. I am very disappointed in you right now. Try to help me understand why you thought it was OK to cheat?
5. I got a call from your teacher today. She claims that you were caught cheating. Do you know what that's about or why she'd think that? I want to hear your side of the story, so I promise not to get mad. The more honest you are with me, the better able I am to help you figure out what to do next.
6. I just read some overwhelming statistics about teens and cheating. What are your thoughts about cheating? Do a lot of kids at your school cheat? Why do you think they do?
7. I want to trust you, but I seriously question your judgment right now. What would you do if you were me right now?
8. I'm trying to understand why you felt compelled to cheat? Are you feeling a lot of pressure to get good grades? Am I making you feel that way? I want you to know that it's far more important to me that you learn and make an effort to do your best than to get straight A's.
9. If you are caught cheating it'll be harder to trust you and you'll be labeled a cheater, even if you never cheat again.
10. If you feel the need to cheat in school it shows that you need help in that subject. Getting help should curb the urge to cheat and help you succeed in the long run.
11. If you make cheating a habit now, you'll never learn how to work hard or develop the skills you need to be successful in college and your career.

12. If you're struggling in a class or on a certain topic, please let me know and we'll get you extra help if necessary. Cheating is never the answer. It cheats you out of learning and growing and it cheats your peers that have studied hard to get the same grade.
13. Is there a lot of competition among your classmates/friends to do well? Do you feel like you can't keep up with them?
14. It is never too late to come clean about cheating. There will be consequences, but when you admit to cheating you already have taken the first step toward making amends and others will respect that.
15. When you cheat in school the short-term reward may be a good grade, but in the long run you're just denying yourself knowledge and the satisfaction of achievement.
16. You did something ethically wrong, but I want to give you the chance to make it right. How do you plan on doing that?
17. You made a bad choice and now you have to live with the consequences of that, whatever those may be. I love you and I'll be here for you, but I'm not going to bail you out of this.
18. Your friend is really putting you in a tough position by saying you're not a true friend if you don't let him copy off of you. That doesn't sound right to me.

Did You Know?

Most teens (80 percent) feel that in order to survive in the world or get ahead, they are going to have to lie or cheat at some point, and 53 percent surveyed said that cheating is "no big deal." So don't assume your teen doesn't cheat, even if she is a star pupil. Educators say that most cheaters come from the top of the class, because those students feel more pressure to succeed and will do anything not to fail. In addition to fear of failure, teens cheat because they are unmotivated to work hard or they feel pressured by their peers.[13]

Talking Tip

What constitutes cheating?

1. Copying off of someone else's test
2. Copying someone else's homework
3. Getting an advanced copy of a test
4. Having someone else do your homework or take a test for you
5. Helping someone else cheat
6. Using a cheat sheet or cell phone to get answers
7. Using other's work or answers on tests

Related Tools

- Behavior Agreement
- Homework Agreement

Related Chapters

- Buy More Time to Respond
- Challenge a Sense of Entitlement
- Clarify the Facts
- Coax Your Teen to Open Up to You
- Confront a Teen Who's Lying
- Encourage Accountability
- Enforce Rules and Consequences
- Tackle Tough Topics
- Peer Pressure
- Stress/Pressure to Succeed

5 Power Phrases about Cutting and Self-Harm

"In truth you like the pain. You like it because you believe you deserve it." —Teenager, online post

1. Have you tried to stop cutting? I know it can be really hard to quit once you start. I care about you so much and want to help you conquer this before it gets out of control and you hurt yourself permanently.
2. Honey, I had no idea that you were feeling so depressed. The only way to relieve the pain is to talk about what is going on. I would love for you to talk to me, but if you don't feel comfortable doing that, I'd like to make an appointment for you to talk to a professional. What would you like to do?
3. What situations make you want to cut? What can you do instead of cutting, the next time that happens? How can you distract yourself? The more you wait out the urge without giving in, the more your urges will decrease over time.
4. You must be going through a really tough time right now. Can you explain to me how cutting helps? I love you too much to let you continue hurting yourself like that. What would you do if someone you loved was putting herself in danger?
5. You must really be hurting inside to turn to cutting. I know the physical pain may help drown out your bad feelings momentarily, but it won't make them go away. Can you tell me what is going on? I'd like to help you find other ways to make yourself feel better that don't harm you physically.

Did You Know?

Cutting has been referred to as the new anorexia among today's teens. It is estimated that 1 in 12 teens deliberately hurt themselves, most often by cutting or burning their own flesh.[14] It usually starts when they're between the ages of 10 and 16 years old and can become addictive.

Talking Tip

Cutting is a way that some teens cope with strong emotional pain caused by:

- Alienation
- Anger
- Depression
- Emptiness
- Frustration
- Hurt
- Loss
- Shame

Related Tools

- Reliable Resources Cheat Sheet

Related Chapters

- Boost Your Teen's Self-Esteem
- Coax Your Teen to Open Up to You
- Comfort Your Teen
- Say "I Love You"
- Tackle Tough Topics
- Body Image
- Depression
- Eating Disorders
- Peer Pressure
- Shyness/Insecurity
- Stress/Pressure to Succeed
- Suicide and Suicidal Thoughts

28 Power Phrases about Dating and Relationships

"I'm not the girl who always has a boyfriend. I'm the girl who rarely has a boyfriend."—Taylor Swift

1. Are any of your friends dating? What are their relationships like? Would you want to be in a relationship like theirs? What would you want in a relationship?
2. Are you comfortable telling the person you're dating how far you're willing to take the relationship and what your physical boundaries are?
3. At what age do you think people should start dating? Why?
4. Do a lot of kids at your school date?
5. Do you have a <boy/girlfriend> right now? How long have you been dating? Are you exclusive?
6. Do you think there should be rules about dating at your age?
7. Do you want to date because your friends are dating or because you really like that person?
8. Have any of your friends started dating? What do you think about that?
9. How do you define dating? What does a typical date look like at your school?
10. How do you know who's dating whom at your school?
11. How long do you think most relationships last at your school?
12. I hear you talking about <name> a lot. When do I get to meet her/him?
13. I think it's important to wait until <age> to start dating because … What do you think?
14. I'm OK with you dating, but I think it's important to lay down some ground rules to make sure you are safe. Want to come up with them together?
15. I've noticed that you and <name> have been spending a lot of time together lately. Are you two dating? What does that mean to you?

16. If you are planning on spending a lot of time with <name>, I want to meet her/him. Can s/he come over for dinner on <date>?
17. Is it common for people at your school to date one person exclusively or to date a lot of people at once?
18. Is s/he kind to you? Does s/he respect you? Do you feel good about yourself when you're with her/him? What do your friends think about her/him?
19. Is there anyone you're interested in dating? What do you like about her/him?
20. It's important to date different people when you're young so that when you're ready to settle down years from now, you'll know what you're looking for.
21. It's important to know before you go out what you're comfortable with so that you can communicate that with your date. Are you comfortable holding hands? Kissing? Touching? Once you know your limits, you need to be strong and secure enough to say "no" or "stop" if things are getting too hot and heavy.
22. The more <boys/girls> you know as friends, the better you'll recognize the right one when s/he comes along later.
23. What types of things do you and <boy/girlfriend> like to do together?
24. What would happen if you got dumped? Could you handle it or would you fall apart? On the flip side, if *you* were the one having to do the breaking up, could you do it in a firm, but kind way?
25. What's the difference between dating and hanging out? What do most of your friends do?
26. Why do you like this person? Do you have common interests? Is s/he kind?
27. Why do you want a <boy/girlfriend> right now?
28. Why do you want to date now?

Did You Know?

The average age that girls start group dating is 12½, boys 13½.[15] Many experts recommend waiting until your teen is 16 before allowing her to go on one-to-one dates, but that is a generalization. Rather than picking an age when your teen can automatically date, consider her maturity level, trustworthiness, and ability to handle the responsibility.

Talking Tip

Your teen is less likely to rebel against your dating guidelines if he is able to help define them. However, if your teen is not willing to have an open, productive discussion about dating with you, he may need a bit more time to mature before entering the complicated world of romantic relationships.

Related Tools

- Dating Agreement

Related Chapters

- Challenge a Sense of Entitlement
- Enforce Rules and Consequences
- Tackle Tough Topics
- Breaking Up and Broken Hearts
- Peer Pressure
- Popularity
- Sex: Abstinence
- Sex: Answers to Common Questions
- Sex: Birth Control
- Sex: Starting "The Talk"
- Toxic Relationships and Abuse

16 Power Phrases about Death and Dying

"What we have once enjoyed we can never lose. All that we love deeply becomes a part of us."—Helen Keller

1. I am so sorry for your pain.
2. I heard that <person's name> died. Do you want to talk about it?
3. I heard your friend died. I'm here if you need me (and even if you don't).
4. I know <person's name> meant a lot to you. I can't imagine how much you're hurting right now. Do you want to talk about it now?
5. I know, it's hard for me to believe it too.
6. I'm so very sorry that you lost <person's name>.
7. I'm here for you if you want someone to talk to or just sit with. I love you.
8. I'm not sure what to say, but I want you to know I love you.
9. Is there anything you want to do to honor <person's name>? I can help.
10. It's OK to cry and it's OK to hurt.
11. Sometimes it helps to put your feelings into words. Do you want to try to write about <person's name> and the ways you're reacting to losing him?
12. Tell me about <person's name>.
13. What are you going to miss most about <person's name>?
14. What did <person's name> mean to you?
15. What is your favorite story about <person's name>?
16. You're feeling <emotion> right now. That's OK. It's a normal part of the grieving process. You may feel that way for a while, and that's OK too. It's tough to believe it now, but eventually you will start feeling better.

Did You Know?

Although there is no "right" way to mourn, Elisabeth Kübler-Ross identified five common stages of grief[16]:

1. Denial and isolation
2. Anger
3. Bargaining
4. Depression
5. Acceptance

Talking Tip

What NOT to say to someone who's grieving:

- Are you feeling better today?
- I know how you feel.
- It is God's will.
- It was his time.
- It's time to get on with your life.
- She's in a better place now.
- You have to be strong.
- You shouldn't feel that way.

Related Chapters

- Coax Your Teen to Open Up to You
- Comfort Your Teen
- Tackle Tough Topics
- Depression

18 Power Phrases about Depression

"The deepest fear we have, 'the fear beneath all fears,' is the fear of not measuring up, the fear of judgment. It's this fear that creates the stress and depression of everyday life." —Tullian Tchividjian

1. Depression is a mental illness that affects your mood and feelings. It is not your fault, and you didn't do anything to cause it. It can make you feel sad, lonely, frustrated, angry, or scared. What questions do you have about depression?
2. Everyone struggles with feelings like these at one time or another. They don't mean you're weak or broken. Accepting your feelings and opening up about them with someone you trust will help you feel less alone.
3. Exercising can do wonders for your mood. It releases a rush of endorphins, which makes you feel instantly happier. Any activity helps, even a short walk. Want to go on one with me?
4. I wanted to check in with you because you haven't seemed yourself lately. Can you tell me what's troubling you?
5. I'd like to take you to see Dr. _______ so that she can help us come up with a plan to make you feel better. This may mean going to therapy on a regular basis or taking medication. Do you have any questions or concerns that you want me or your doctor to address?
6. It's perfectly normal to feel sad or irritable every now and then when you're a teenager. But if these feelings don't go away or become so intense that you can't handle them, you may be suffering from depression. If that's the case, please let me know. There are many things we can do to make you feel better.
7. No matter what it feels like right now, people love and care about you.
8. Recently, I have noticed some differences in you and wondered how you are doing. How can I best support you right now?

9. Some people think that talking about sad feelings will make them worse, but the opposite is almost always true. It is very helpful to share your worries with someone who will listen and care—like me.
10. Talking about your feelings with someone you trust may help you feel better. I am always here to talk to you about anything or you may want to talk to some of your friends. Which of your friends do you think you might be able to talk to about your feelings?
11. When you're depressed, you may not feel like seeing anybody or doing anything. Just getting out of bed in the morning may be difficult. But isolating yourself only makes depression worse and being around people may make you feel better. What can you do to stay social, even if it's the last thing you want to do?
12. You are not alone and your depression is not a hopeless case. Even though it may feel like no one understands you, depression is far more common in teens than you may think and there are many treatments we can look into that will help you feel better. Do you want to do that?
13. You may be tempted to drink or use drugs in an effort to escape from your feelings and get a "mood boost," even if just for a short time. However, drinking and taking drugs will actually make you feel worse—not better. In fact, they often cause people to feel depressed in the first place.
14. You may have heard people say hurtful or inaccurate things about people with mental illness or depression. Occasionally, when people don't understand something, they'll say something hurtful or make incorrect judgments.
15. You seem like you're really down, and not yourself. I want to help you. Is there anything I can do?
16. You seem pretty down these days. When I'm feeling bad, it always helps me to talk to someone.
17. You shouldn't be embarrassed about having depression or feel like you have to hide it, but you should only tell people who you trust and know will be supportive. Who do you feel comfortable telling? Is there anyone who you would like me to tell or be sure NOT to tell?

18. You're not alone in this.

Did You Know?

Your teen may be depressed if he:

1. Can't concentrate
2. Constantly feels irritable, sad, or angry
3. Cries about everything
4. Doesn't want to do the things he used to love to do
5. Lacks energy or is easily fatigued
6. Has frequent headaches or physical problems
7. Has gained or lost a substantial amount of weight
8. Sleeps too much or not enough
9. Talks about being bad, ugly, stupid, or worthless
10. Withdraws from friends and family

Talking Tip

4 things to remember when talking to your depressed teen:

1. Be gentle but persistent.
2. Listen without lecturing.
3. Offer support.
4. Validate her feelings.

Related Tools

- Reliable Resources Cheat Sheet

Related Chapters

- Boost Your Teen's Self-Esteem
- Coax Your Teen to Open Up to You
- Comfort Your Teen

- Say "I Love You"
- Tackle Tough Topics
- Breaking Up and Broken Hearts
- Cutting and Self-Harm
- Eating Disorders
- Stress/Pressure to Succeed
- Suicide and Suicidal Thoughts

16 Power Phrases about Divorce

"I don't see divorce as a failure. I see it as the end to a story. In a story, everything has an end and a beginning." —Olga Kurylenko

1. Feeling sad or angry about this is OK and completely justified. This is tough on all of us.
2. I understand that you're <emotion> about the divorce. I am too.
3. I'm sure you know that we both love you very much. Just because your <dad/mom> and I have decided not to live with each other anymore doesn't mean that we don't want to be with you.
4. If you have any questions, you can ask them now, or you can talk to me or <dad/mom> later at any time. Remember, we'll always be there for you, and we love you very much.
5. It's OK to feel <emotion> about our divorce. You have every right to. To be honest, I'm feeling pretty <emotion> about it too.
6. Just because your <dad/mom> and I are getting divorced doesn't mean we will love you any less. Quite the opposite. We will love you no matter what.
7. Our decision to split up is completely due to issues between us. It is absolutely not because of something you did or didn't do. I want to make sure you understand that.
8. Parents can divorce each other, but they do not ever divorce their kids. We'll be your mom and dad forever.
9. Part of the divorce process may require you to go to court. The judge is there to help you decide which parent you should live with during the school year and how long to visit the other parent during the summers and weekends. Do you have any concerns?
10. Sometimes during a divorce the parents argue with each other and say things that aren't true, out of anger. We are going to do our very best not to do that. But if we trip up, know that it's because this is very painful for us and we are reacting to our hurt.
11. This must be really hard for you.

12. We both love you very, very much and always will. That never changes.
13. We know that you've heard us fighting a lot, and here's why ...
14. What don't I have here that would make you more comfortable when you come over?
15. You have done nothing to cause us to divorce. It is not your fault. This is between your <dad/mom> and me. There is nothing you could have done to change what happened.
16. You may feel like this is all <my/mom's/dad's> fault, but you don't know the full story. There are other ways of looking at what happened. When you're not so <emotion>, let's talk more about it.

Did You Know?

The divorce rate in America is 40 to 50 percent for first marriages, 60 percent for second marriages and 73 percent for third marriages. The average length of divorce proceedings is a year.[17]

Talking Tip

Be prepared to answer the following questions from your teen:

- Can I continue my <activities>?
- Can I still go to camp next summer?
- Can I still see my friends?
- How will you share parenting responsibilities?
- Is there a chance you'll get back together?
- Was it something I did?
- What will we do on <holiday>?
- Where will I keep all my stuff?
- Where will I live?
- Where will I spend my summer?
- Where will our dog or cat live?
- Who decides where I live?

- Why did you divorce?
- Will I still go to the same school?
- Will there be enough money?
- Will you and <mom/dad> still live in the same town?
- Will you continue to coach my soccer or Little-League team?
- Will you still spend time with me?

Related Chapters

- Coax Your Teen to Open Up to You
- Comfort Your Teen
- Make Your Teen Feel Valued
- Say "I Love You"
- Say "I'm Sorry" with Conviction
- Tackle Tough Topics

16 Power Phrases about Driving

"Baseball is like driving, it's the one who gets home safely that counts."—Tommy Lasorda

1. Because I love you and need you to be safe, I want to make sure you fully understand the implications of driving under the influence of alcohol or drugs. First, it puts you at a far greater risk of getting into a serious, even fatal, accident. Second, you'd face serious consequences for breaking the law. That includes a trip to jail, the loss of your driver's license, and dozens of other expenses. You could also risk losing academic eligibility, college acceptance, scholarship awards, and more.
2. Before I give you the keys, remind me what the driving rules are.
3. How do you think your friends would react if you asked them to quiet down or stop distracting you while you were driving?
4. How many friends do you think it's OK to have in your car when you're driving? I just want you to be aware that every person you have in your car increases your risk of getting into an accident.
5. I know it's tempting to talk or text when you're driving or at least glance at your phone when you hear a message come through. But it only takes a split second to rear-end a car or miss a street sign or light. How can you make sure that you stay off your phone when you're in the driver's seat? What can you do if you have to make or answer a call?
6. I know you're really excited to be driving. I'm excited for you too. But it's also a huge responsibility, so I want to lay out some ground rules for you. Let's walk through them and let me know if you have any questions or concerns.
7. I remember when I first got my driver's license. The sense of freedom that I had was indescribable, but it also was a lot of added pressure and responsibility. How do you feel about driving?

8. I want to remind you that driving is a privilege—a privilege that you will lose if you don't drive by our rules, which are ... These rules are set in place for your safety, so they are nonnegotiable. But as long as you follow them and show me that you're responsible, you'll have access to the car as we agreed.
9. If you find yourself in a situation where you feel unsafe or uncomfortable, I'd like you to call me. Can you promise me that? Are there any reasons that you can think of that would prevent you from calling me?
10. If you're not ready to talk about how to keep yourself, your passengers, and other drivers safe, then you're not ready for the keys to the car. Let me know when you're ready.
11. So, what do you think about driving so far? Is it as awesome as you expected?
12. The simplest way to prevent getting hurt in a car crash is to buckle up. How do you remember to put your seatbelt on? How can you make sure everyone in your car wears a seatbelt at all times?
13. What is the best part of having your driver's license? The worst?
14. What would you do if you got a ride with a friend and she spent the whole time talking rather than watching the road?
15. Which one of your friends is the best driver? Worst? Craziest? Why?
16. Your birthday is coming up, which means you can get your permit. I am so excited for you, but first I want us to all talk and establish some ground rules and go over safety.

Did You Know?

Teens whose parents talk with them about driving safety, and require them to sign driving contracts, are less likely to die in a car crash.[18]

Talking Tip

7 Driving Rules Every Teen Should Know

1. Absolutely no alcohol.
2. Always buckle up.
3. No talking or texting while driving.
4. No more than one passenger at a time.
5. Obey all speed limits and traffic laws.
6. Have the car back in the driveway by <time>.
7. Contribute to <gas/insurance/maintenance/etc.>.

Related Tools

- Reliable Resources Cheat Sheet
- Driving Agreement

Related Chapters

- Challenge a Sense of Entitlement
- Encourage Accountability
- Enforce Rules and Consequences
- Give Constructive Feedback
- Grab (and Keep) Your Teen's Attention
- Prompt Your Teen to Problem-Solve

12 Power Phrases about Eating Disorders

(Anorexia and Bulimia)

"I am forever engaged in a silent battle in my head over whether or not to lift the fork to my mouth, and when I talk myself into doing so, I taste only shame. I have an eating disorder." —Jena Morrow

1. Do you make yourself sick because you feel uncomfortably full? Do you worry that you have lost control over how much you eat? Do you believe yourself to be fat when others say that you are too thin? Would you say that food dominates your life? (Note: Yes to two or more questions indicates a possible eating disorder.)
2. I feel like you've been <warning sign> lately. I'm worried that this is a sign that you're going through something really tough right now. What's been going on?
3. I know this is difficult and you don't want to discuss it, but we need to talk about your weight and eating habits.
4. I know when I feel out of control in some areas of my life, I try to gain more control in others, like my weight. Do you ever do that?
5. I love you and your well-being is important to me. Lately I've noticed <warning sign/s> and I'm concerned about you. I'd like to make an appointment for you to talk to a professional about this. Will you go—if for no other reason than to put my mind at ease?
6. I may be completely overreacting, but I'll never forgive myself if I don't bring it up and something bad happens to you. I've noticed that <warning sign>. Can we talk about it?
7. I noticed that you haven't been eating <carbs/fats/etc.> lately. Why are you cutting back on these types of foods?
8. I scheduled an appointment with your doctor to explore what's going on with your weight and overall health. We need to make sure you're healthy.
9. I'm concerned about you because you refuse to eat <lunch/dinner>.

10. I've noticed that you've been making negative comments about your body and talking about losing weight. How do you feel about your body right now?
11. It makes me afraid to hear you vomiting.
12. You probably think that what you eat isn't any of my business, but the truth is I'm concerned about you. You're my <daughter/son> and I love you and want to help you. Since I don't know exactly what to do, I made an appointment with a doctor who can help.

Did You Know?

Your teen may have an eating disorder if she exhibits several of the following warning signs:

- Develops unusual eating habits
- Disappears after meals
- Exercises excessively
- Experiences irregular menstrual cycles
- Has a distorted body image
- Overeats when distressed
- Skips most meals
- Uses laxatives or diuretics frequently
- Weighs herself frequently

Talking Tip

If your teen is struggling with an eating disorder, avoid:

1. Complimenting her weight loss ("You're so thin. I'm jealous. I wish I could lose weight like that.")
2. Getting angry or forceful. ("Enough! You need to stop this nonsense right now and eat.")
3. Giving simple solutions. ("Why don't you just eat a sandwich?")
4. Insulting her. ("You look like a skeleton. I can see your bones.")

5. Lecturing or nagging. ("If you don't stop this, you're going to do serious damage to your body.")
6. Shaming and blaming. ("If you loved me, then you would eat this food." "Quit feeling sorry for yourself.")

Related Tools

- Reliable Resources Cheat Sheet
- Suicide Warning Signs Cheat Sheet

Related Chapters

- Boost Your Teen's Self-Esteem
- Coax Your Teen to Open Up to You
- Comfort Your Teen
- Tackle Tough Topics
- Body Image
- Cutting and Self-Harm
- Peer Pressure
- Stress/Pressure to Succeed
- Substance Abuse
- Suicide and Suicidal Thoughts

7 Power Phrases about Excessive Behavior

(Gaming, Internet Use, TV, Texting, etc.)

"Anything that you can become obsessed with, and you do so much that you don't do the things you need to do with family, friends, school, job—that can be an addiction. And texting absolutely can qualify." —Dale Archer

1. How does <behavior> make you feel? Does it make you feel good about yourself? Is there anything else that makes you feel that way?
2. How much time a day do you think you spend <behavior>? Do you think that's healthy? Do you think you can cut back on it? By how much?
3. I know you really enjoy <behavior>, but I'm sad that you're missing out on a lot of the other wonderful experiences life has to offer. I want to work with you to come up with a plan to find more balance in your life.
4. I'm concerned that important things and people in your life are getting neglected or hurt because you spend so much of your time <behavior>. I care about you and want to help you establish a healthier balance. Let's sit down at <time> to come up with a plan.
5. What do you get out of <behavior>? What skills are you developing? How do you plan on applying those skills to everyday life? Are there other ways to develop those skills that are more <active/social/etc.>?
6. What do you think will happen if you go a hour/day/week without <behavior>?
7. You <behavior> so much, I'm worried that you are using it to distract you from something that's really bothering you. What's going on?

Did You Know?

Your teen may be addicted to an activity if he:

- Gets irritable when trying to cut down on it

- Lets it interfere with homework and other obligations
- Lies to friends and family to conceal it
- Spends increasing amounts of time doing it
- Spends less time with family and friends because of it
- Thinks about it during other activities
- Uses it to escape from real-life problems, anxiety, or depression

Talking Tip

Studies have found that the more time teens spend alone with their fathers, the higher their self-esteem. Yet, on average, American teens spend 70 times more time in front of the TV, video games, and computer than they do talking with their dads. So dads, turn off the TV and sit down with your teen for some quality one-on-one time—today.[19]

Related Tools

- Behavior Agreement
- Cell Phone Agreement
- Internet Use Agreement

Related Chapters

- Challenge a Sense of Entitlement
- Encourage Accountability
- Enforce Rules and Consequences
- Motivate Your Teen
- Persuade Your Teen to Do Something
- Tackle Tough Topics
- Technology Use and Safety
- Underachievement

17 Power Phrases about Extreme Emotions

(Outbursts, Aggression and Mood Swings)

"The trick is to be grateful when your mood is high and graceful when it is low." —Richard Carlson

1. Although anger is a normal, healthy emotion, it can get in the way of getting what you want. Learning to channel your emotion in a productive way can be a lot more effective. Can you think of some ways you can use your anger for your benefit?
2. Although I understand keeping your emotions in check can be a challenge, please understand that your negative mood impacts the rest of the family. I'm here to listen if you want to talk about it. Otherwise, I'd really appreciate it if you work on managing your mood somewhere away from the family, like your room. We'd love to have you join us again once you are calm and can be nicer to us.
3. Are there certain things that you know bother you or make you feel <negative emotion>? Can you avoid any of them? What are some ways you can control your reaction and remain calm the next time you encounter one of your triggers?
4. Clearly you need to vent. I'm going to give you 10 minutes to get it all off your chest. Let your thoughts rip. Ready? Go. [Note: You may want to add the requirement that he refrains from personal insults, profanity, and physical violence, etc., if necessary].
5. Do you ever find yourself getting really irritable for almost no reason? Or suddenly feeling down without knowing why? This emotional roller-coaster actually is common during puberty. The hormones your body is now producing <estrogen and progesterone in girls and testosterone in boys> not only cause physical changes but may cause emotional changes as well. That's what causes the ups and downs that sometimes make you feel out of control.

6. Everything may take on a new and more intense meaning when you're going through puberty. Your hormones may make you feel things more deeply or make it difficult for you to control your emotions. You can go from feeling completely happy to extremely sad in a matter of minutes. This can be confusing, but just know that it's normal and that the feelings will even out in time.
7. How do you feel after you've vented your anger? Are you ever rewarded for reacting in anger or do you end up paying the consequences?
8. I can't talk to you when you're this emotional. I'm going to come back after we've both calmed down and we can talk then.
9. I know you're <emotion>, how can I help?
10. I'm getting frustrated—I'm going to take a break.
11. I'm going for a <walk/run/bike ride/etc.>, want to join me?
12. It's not necessarily what happens in your life that makes you emotional; it's how your brain reacts to what's happening in your life. Hopefully you'll take some comfort knowing that your moodiness is the result of your brain chemistry rather than a flaw in your personality.
13. Next time you get mad, try taking a deep breath, stepping away from the situation, and asking yourself, "Why am I really mad?" Often people get angry at the little things, when it's really a much bigger issue that's upsetting them.
14. The good news is, as fast as you can get into a bad mood, you can also get out of one.
15. There's nothing wrong with crying; in fact, it may actually make you feel better.
16. Think about the last time you reacted in anger. Would a better response have earned you more respect from others? Did your actions result in positive change, negative change, or no change at all?
17. You seem really upset. What's going on?

Did You Know?

The adolescent brain is primed to learn, which makes the teen years the most opportune time to teach self-regulation, impulse control and anger-management skills.

Talking Tip

When your teen is overly emotional, don't:

1. Get emotional too—it'll just add fuel to the fire
2. Get physical—violence begets more violence, not resolution
3. Give in—this only rewards your teen's negative behavior
4. Try to reason—until he's calm, it'll just make your teen more upset
5. Punish his anger—instead give consequences for his behavior (e.g., swearing, destroying property, etc.)

Quick Trick

If your teen exhibits several of the following behaviors consistently for six months or more across several venues (e.g., home, school, work), s/he may have Oppositional Defiant Disorder (ODD). If so, seek professional help immediately.

1. Acting annoyed, angry, resentful, spiteful or vindictive
2. Arguing with adults
3. Blaming others for his misbehavior
4. Defying or refusing to comply with rules
5. Losing his temper
6. Purposefully annoying other people

Related Tools

- Reliable Resources Cheat Sheet

- Suicide Warning Signs Cheat Sheet
- Behavior Agreement

Related Chapters

- Address Your Teen's Disrespect
- Buy More Time to Respond
- Challenge a Sense of Entitlement
- Cool Down a Heated Situation
- Encourage Accountability
- Enforce Rules and Consequences
- Respond to Arguing
- Bullying Others

20 Power Phrases about Homosexuality

(Am I Gay?)

"As a child, recognizing my difference from other kids, I went to the local public library to try to better understand my reality. Back then, many library card catalogues didn't even list 'homosexuality' as a topic." —James McGreevey

1. A lot of kids your age are trying to figure things out. That's perfectly normal. I'm ready to listen to anything you have to say if you want to talk it out with me.
2. Allowing ourselves to be confused or unsure about our sexuality is an important way of giving ourselves time to deal with who we are as sexual beings. When you are ready, pay attention to the signals of attraction from your body and your brain. They won't lead you astray.
3. Be proud of who you are and be free to be whatever you want to be without anyone telling you how you should act or dress or talk or walk.
4. For many teens, thinking about and/or experimenting with the same sex may cause concerns and anxiety regarding their sexual orientation, but it's completely normal.
5. Having fleeting feelings about or even having a sexual experience with a person of the same sex doesn't necessarily mean that a person is gay or bisexual. In fact, it's quite common for people to experiment with their sexuality, especially during adolescence and young adulthood.
6. How long have you been having these feelings? Are they new or have you had them for a while?
7. I have an idea. Why don't you write down a list of the 10 people that you find most attractive (boy or girl). Now look at the list. What does that tell you?

8. I just want to let you know that if you're having feelings that are different from other <boys/girls> it's OK to tell me because there's nothing you can say to me that's going to make me any less proud of you, or love you any less.
9. If you're having overpowering thoughts and only think about people of the same sex, then yes, there is a chance that you are gay. If that's the case, there is no reason to feel bad or guilty. We'll work through it together.
10. It is perfectly normal for teens to question their sexual orientation. However, having a crush on someone of the same sex at your age doesn't necessarily mean you're gay. Take some time to explore your feelings before you define yourself.
11. It may be too early to know if you're gay. You're just beginning to explore your sexual attraction for other people. It could be of the opposite sex or the same sex. These feelings may change as time goes on. Whichever end up being the strongest, it's OK. I will love you no matter what.
12. It may help to think of sexual orientation as a spectrum, or to think of yourself as loving *people*, not just their gender.
13. It's normal to be unsure about your sexuality at your age. You're still experimenting and defining who you are, so don't feel pressured to label yourself as gay or straight right now.
14. It's normal, and fairly common, for teens to experiment with same-sex friends. It doesn't mean they're gay, just curious.
15. Many teens worry that they might be homosexual at one point or another. It's because they are still exploring their sexuality.
16. OK, so you kissed someone of the same sex. How did it make you feel? What does it mean to you?
17. Some people know early on if they are straight or gay. Others take a while to determine what makes them happy and comfortable. You will figure it out in your own time. I just want you to know that I will love you and accept you no matter what.

18. There are many degrees of sexual orientation, and if you find you don't fit easily into one category, perhaps you are bisexual. Don't label yourself until you're ready and willing to be.
19. You are not alone in this struggle. There are many gay, lesbian, bisexual, and straight people all over the world who have been in your situation. The doubt. The nagging guilt. The uncertainty. They've all been through it.
20. You don't have to label yourself if you don't want to. You like whom you like, and leave it at that.

Did You Know?

One out of 10 teens may be gay, lesbian, bisexual, or transgender, and many come out as early as 11 or 12 years old. If a teen's family rejects him after coming out, the teen is nine times more likely to attempt suicide.[20]

Talking Tip

If you feel uncomfortable or unequipped for talking to your teen about her sexuality, you can contact the Trevor Project, an organization for LGBT youth. (24-hour helpline: 1-866-488-7386; website and online community: http://www.thetrevorproject.org.)

Related Tools

- Reliable Resources Cheat Sheet

Related Chapters

- Buy More Time to Respond
- Boost Your Teen's Self-Esteem
- Say "I Love You"
- Tackle Tough Topics
- Homosexuality (Coming Out)

- Peer Pressure
- Puberty (Boys)
- Puberty (Girls)
- Sex: Answers to Common Questions
- Sex: Starting "The Talk"
- Tolerance

20 Power Phrases about Homosexuality

(Coming Out)

"Everybody's journey is individual. If you fall in love with a boy, you fall in love with a boy. The fact that many Americans consider it a disease says more about them than it does about homosexuality." —James A. Baldwin

1. All I care about is that you're happy.
2. Although it's not something I would choose for you because of all the obstacles that I know you'll face because of it, I know you don't have a choice.
3. Being gay, lesbian, bisexual, transgender or anything in-between is OK. No one should make you feel bad about who you are inside. I love you and respect you for who you are, no matter what. If your friends are your true friends, they'll love you no matter what.
4. From now on, whatever you decide to do, you're not in this alone. I will support you.
5. Have you found a support group to help you through this? If not, I can help you find one.
6. Have you met someone already? When can I meet <her/him>?
7. Have you thought about who else you are going to tell? I support you, but not everyone will be as accepting about this.
8. I appreciate you telling me. I've got to be honest; I'm having trouble wrapping my head around this right now. I need some time to process before I'm ready to talk about it. But know that I still love you, and nothing you say will change that.
9. I can't imagine how scary it is to come out, especially when you don't know how people will react. I'm proud of you.
10. I love you just the same, and you're the same <son/daughter> to me that you were five minutes ago.
11. I really admire you for telling me. It must have taken a lot of courage for you to accept this and open up about it. I'm here for you.

12. If you're to the point of telling me you're gay, you must be sure. How long have you known this?
13. People will react to the news that you're gay in many different ways. Hopefully most won't care. Some already might have guessed. But there will be others who can't or won't accept it. I worry about how those people might mistreat you. Please know that I am on your side and will help in any way I can.
14. Since it is well known that teens want to fit in with their peers, you should ask yourself if it makes sense that they would choose a lifestyle that alienates them from their peer group.
15. Thank you for telling me. I love you for who you are, and that won't change.
16. Thank you for trusting me with something so personal. I love you. What can I do to support you?
17. Try not to think of your new sexual revelation as a burden; instead, think of it as liberation. There is nothing wrong with being gay. You are not any less of a person for being who you are.
18. You're not alone in this. I am always here for you.
19. You're not alone. There are literally millions of other kids out there who've been where you are now. You need to find them and help each other.
20. Your sexuality isn't a choice, but when, how, and to whom you come out is. Take some time to get comfortable with yourself first and then it'll be easier to allow other people to go through their process of understanding.

Did You Know?

There are many places to find support for you and your teen:

- Gay, Lesbian and Straight Education Network (GLSEN): www.glsen.org
- High school gay-straight alliances
- Lyric: lyric.org

- Parents, Families and Friends of Lesbians and Gays (PFLAG): www.pflag.org
- Trevor Project: www.thetrevorproject.org

Talking Tip

Ask your teen *before* you "come out" to others on her behalf.

Related Tools

- Reliable Resources Cheat Sheet

Related Chapters

- Buy More Time to Respond
- Boost Your Teen's Self-Esteem
- Coax Your Teen to Open Up to You
- Tackle Tough Topics
- Being Bullied
- Homosexuality (Am I Gay?)
- Peer Pressure
- Puberty (Boys)
- Puberty (Girls)
- Sex: Answers to Common Questions
- Sex: STDs
- Tolerance

14 Power Phrases about Hygiene

(or Lack Thereof)

"People often say that motivation doesn't last. Well, neither does bathing—that's why we recommend it daily." —Zig Ziglar

1. As you get older, your hormones affect your sweat glands, which can lead your body to smell a bit more and to smell differently. When that happens, it's time to start wearing deodorant and showering more often to keep your body feeling and smelling clean.
2. By now, you've probably noticed hair growing in different places on your body. If you want to shave, talk to me. I can help you find the right razor and shaving cream.
3. Can you explain to me why you don't want to <shower/brush teeth/change underwear/etc.>? What don't you like about it?
4. Douching actually does more harm than good. It is better to wash your vagina regularly with warm water and unscented soaps. Also, avoid scented tampons, pads, and powders—they can cause or increase vaginal infections.
5. During puberty the pores in your skin produce more oil, especially on your face. This can cause acne. You may have to wash your hair and face more often now. Do you want me to help you come up with a skin care routine?
6. Growing up means that you have to be responsible for taking good care of your body. That means you have to shower or bathe every day and after exercising; wear clean underwear and socks every day; brush and floss your teeth twice a day; wear deodorant or antiperspirant, etc.
7. I am not telling you this to hurt your feelings, but I'd want to know if I was in your shoes. Your body is starting to emit an odor. This is a healthy sign that you're maturing, but we need to talk about ways to manage it.

8. I'm telling you this because it's important for you to know. Now that you're getting older, you need to be hypervigilant about staying clean. Your body is now producing more oils and bacteria, which can cause acne, greasy hair, and body odor. If you like, I can share the names of some products and strategies that have worked well for me.
9. Sweating is a normal and healthy response to heat, physical activity, stress, anxiety, and nervousness.
10. The best way to control body odor is to stay clean and dry. Shower or bathe every day and change into clean underwear and clothing whenever you become sweaty.
11. When you take a shower, it's important to wash and carefully dry five body zones: feet, face, hands, armpits, and bottom, to reduce the bacteria that causes body odor.
12. When you were little, you didn't have to take as many showers, but now you might notice that if you skip a day or two, you feel grimy and gross. That's because your body is going through changes that make it necessary for you to pay extra close attention to your hygiene, and that means taking showers more regularly.
13. You have been sweating since you were born, but now that you're a teen, your sweat glands are more active and secrete certain chemicals that can cause the body to have an odor. It's important to start showering more and wearing deodorant to prevent your body odor from overpowering the people around you.
14. You're now at the age to start using deodorant like an adult. Do you want to go to the store with me to pick it out or would you prefer that I just get you what I think is best?

Did You Know?

Your teen's refusal to maintain good hygiene may actually be more about winning a power struggle than not wanting to be clean. The more you try to control your teen and push him to do what you want (e.g., shower, change clothes, etc.) the more he is going to push back and refuse. As difficult (and stinky) as it may be, it's more effective to back off and let your teen experience the uncomfortable natural consequences.

Talking Tip

Give your teen a "welcome to adolescence" CARE Package, and walk him through each product explaining what it's for and how to use it. To make it more appealing, buy teen-friendly products and put them in a fun-but-inconspicuous container or bag. Some things to include:

- Acne lotion
- Dandruff shampoo and conditioner
- Dental floss
- Deodorant/antiperspirant
- Facial cleanser
- Feminine hygiene products (maxi pads/tampons/panty liners)
- Foot powder
- Moisturizer
- Mouthwash/breath mints/gum
- Nail trimmer
- Nose-hair trimmer
- Perfume/cologne/body spray
- Razor and shaving cream
- Shower poof
- Soap/body wash

Related Tools

- Behavior Agreement

Related Chapters

- Constructive Feedback
- Persuade Your Teen to Do Something

- Tackle Tough Topics
- Appearance
- Puberty (Boys)
- Puberty (Girls)

15 Power Phrases about Learning Disabilities

"I get stubborn and dig in when people tell me I can't do something and I think I can. It goes back to my childhood when I had problems in school because I have a learning disability." —Ann Bancroft

1. Although there's no cure for learning disabilities, you can find strategies to help manage your learning differences so that you can still accomplish your goals and dreams.
2. Do you ever feel like your learning differences impact your confidence and ability to make friends? In what way?
3. Dyslexia makes it hard for people to recognize or process letters and the sounds they make. The most common challenge that they have is mixing up letters and numbers that are similar, for example the letters 'd' and 'b' or 'n' and 'u.' This makes reading, writing, and spelling very challenging.
4. Everyone learns in different ways. Let's keep trying to find the way that works best for you.
5. I know this assignment/task is difficult for you, but I'm confident that you can do it. What can I do to help?
6. I like the way you tried a bunch of different strategies to solve that problem until you found the one that worked best for you.
7. It must be stressful feeling like everyone is evaluating you and you can't show them everything you know. Remember, they're not judging how smart you are, they're just seeing how you learn so they can teach you in a way that's best for you.
8. Just because you have trouble studying for a test doesn't mean that you have a learning disability. You may learn better if you try some different methods. For example, some people learn better by listening, others by writing things down, and others by doing something with their hands. Experiment and see what works best for you.

9. People with ADHD (Attention Deficit Hyperactivity Disorder) often have a hard time focusing long enough to learn and study. They also may be easily distracted, have trouble concentrating, or struggle to stay still and control their impulses.
10. People with learning disabilities are just as intelligent as most of their peers, they just process certain types of information differently. In fact, brilliant and creative people like inventor Alexander Graham Bell, director Steven Spielberg, newscaster Anderson Cooper, designer Tommy Hilfiger, investor Charles Schwab, actor Jim Carrey, and Walt Disney had learning disabilities.
11. Some people's brains have wiring glitches (sort of like having a traffic jam on a major highway), which impacts its ability to receive, process, analyze, or store information. This can make it more difficult to learn as quickly as other people, or to concentrate or focus, because your mind wants to wander.
12. That homework assignment seemed pretty tough. I really admired the way you concentrated and finished it.
13. We all learn at different rates. It may take more time for you to get comfortable with the material, but if you keep up at it like this you will.
14. You just may require more time to process information. That's common. For example, have you ever felt that you didn't understand something in class, but it suddenly become clear later that day? If that's the case, we can get you some help so that you get the time you need.
15. You really studied for that test and your improvement shows it. Your study strategy really worked!

Did You Know?

Research shows that 8 to 10 percent of American children less than 18 years of age have some type of learning disability. At least 20 percent of them have a type of disorder that makes it difficult to focus and around 80 percent have trouble reading.[21]

Talking Tip

Your teen may have a learning disability if he has trouble:

- Adjusting to change.
- Focusing for more than a few minutes.
- Following directions.
- Keeping letters, numbers and sounds straight.
- Memorizing or retaining information.
- Organizing his ideas.
- Putting things in order.
- Sitting still.
- Understanding what he reads.
- With his hand-eye coordination and fine motor skills.

Related Chapters

- Boost Your Teen's Self-Esteem
- Make Your Teen Feel Valued
- Spark Collaboration
- Tackle Tough Topics
- Being Bullied
- Extreme Emotions
- Shyness/Insecurity
- Substance Abuse
- Tolerance

20 Power Phrases about Money

"You are not teaching your 16-year-old child to spend responsibly when you give him a credit card any more than you are teaching gun responsibility by letting him sleep with a loaded automatic weapon with the safety off." —Dave Ramsey

1. Do you want to help me balance the checkbook?
2. Here's $_______ to buy your back-to-school supplies and clothes. Let's work together to create a budget so that you make sure you get all the things you need first. You can buy the fun extras with the money that is left over.
3. I know you want <desired product>. How much is it? One way you could earn that is by doing a few extra jobs for me. For example, I'll pay your $_____ to <task>. Interested?
4. I know you want to buy a <expensive item>. How much does it cost? To give you an extra incentive to save your money, I'm going to match the amount of money you save up to $______. How's that sound?
5. I think it would be great for you to get a part-time job this summer. It'll give you working experience and help you earn enough money to <goal>. Do you need help getting started with your job search?
6. If you use credit cards, or borrow money and pay it off on time and in full every month, you can establish good credit—and not pay extra on everything. Having good credit can make it easier to do things such as get a car loan and rent an apartment when you get out of school.
7. If you want to know how to budget your money, the first thing you can do is write the things you absolutely need in one column and the things you want, but could live without, in another. Add up how much the needed items will cost you and see how much you have left over to spend on items you want.

8. Interested in seeing where the family money goes every month? We earn about $______ a month. From that we have to pay for the mortgage, TV, utilities, food, gas, etc. After we pay all our living costs, we've got about $_____ left over. We try to save $_____ from that and donate at least $______. In the end we've got about $_____ left over. That's why we can't always afford to buy every new gadget out there.
9. Let's say you use your credit card to buy $2,000 worth of stuff (clothes, video games, etc.) Your credit card has an annual percentage rate (APR) of 24.9 percent (show her where to find that on the credit card statement). This is how much interest you have to pay every year. If you don't pay it back that month, you'll end up paying an extra $40.93: $2,000 x 30 *days* x (0.249/365) = $40.93 (Note: 0.249/365=*interest rate/days a year).* So the next month you're paying interest on $2,040.93 and it keeps adding up every month.
10. Now that you have a job, we need to set you up with your own bank account. Let me know when you're free to go to the bank with me.
11. Thank goodness we didn't buy <a wanted item/service>. If we had, we wouldn't have had the money to pay for <a needed item/service>.
12. That's a bummer that you've already spent your allowance for the week and don't have enough to <desired activity/product>. How can you budget your money more wisely next week so you know you'll have enough to do/get the things you want?
13. The one key rule you need to know when it comes to money is that your expenses should never be more than your income.
14. What do you think you could buy with $100? $1,000? $10,000? Let's look up the real costs and see how close you are.
15. What do you want to buy? How much is it? How much do you have saved up so far? So you need $______ more. Let's do some planning on what money you have coming in and what can be set aside to meet your goals.
16. When you make money it's best to divide your earnings into four key areas: saving, spending, investing, and donating.

17. When you use a credit card, you're borrowing money. It's not free money. You not only have to pay it back, but you also have to pay extra, which is called interest. So in the end you end up paying a lot more for something than the original price. The longer it takes you to pay it back, the more interest you have to pay.
18. When you work for a company, the company will take out money from your pay for income taxes. How much they take out is based on how much you make. So the more you make, the more they take. It may seem unfair, but you're actually helping to run our country. Federal income taxes help pay for things like building and repairing national highways, the military, space exploration, law enforcement, and aid to foreign countries.
19. When you write a check you are promising that you have enough money in your bank account for the person/place you're writing the check for to take out. If you write it for more than you have in your bank account, it'll bounce. This means the person/place won't get the money you promised them and you'll also have to pay additional fees and penalties.
20. Why save money? If you put your money into a savings account you'll actually earn more money on it. Credit cards charge you interest, but banks pay you interest. So the more you put into savings, the more money you'll make just by not spending it.

Did You Know?

Nearly a third of high school seniors have a credit card and college freshmen carry almost $1,600 in credit card debt.[22]

Talking Tip

How to teach your teen to be financially responsible:

- Be transparent about your family finances.
- Discuss the difference between "wants" and "needs."

- Encourage your teen to make her own money.
- Give your teen an allowance and a debit card, and then teach him how to manage his own money.
- Help your teen set specific financial goals (e.g., save enough money to buy a specific video game).
- Make your teen pay for her own mistakes (e.g., cell phone replacement).
- Help your teen set up a savings account and encourage him to set money aside.
- Show your teen real-life examples.

Related Tools

- Reliable Resources Cheat Sheet
- Allowance Agreement

Related Chapters

- Challenge a Sense of Entitlement
- Encourage Accountability
- Shoplifting/Stealing

21 Power Phrases about Obesity and Weight

"Parents of teens report that it's easier for them to talk about sex than their kids' weight." —"Raising Fit Kids" national study

1. A lot of people find it difficult to develop a healthier lifestyle, especially if they try to do it alone. Because it's so important and you're so important to me, I want to do it with you. What are some things that can get in our way of eating healthier and exercising more? How do you think we can overcome those obstacles?
2. Are you uncomfortable about <your/my/your siblings> weight? How does it make you feel?
3. Do you feel like you have enough energy to do the things you like to do? Carrying extra weight around means your body has to work harder than it needs to. Do you like it when your teacher gives you extra homework to do? Well your body doesn't like to do more work than it has to either. If we can help your body stop overworking, we can make sure you have enough energy to do things that you like to do, such as …
4. How about we take a <bike ride/walk> together after dinner twice a week? It'll be fun, and we can both get healthier.
5. I know you don't like being heavier than your friends. I'm more concerned about how it affects your health. What can we do to make you healthier and feel more confident?
6. I love you and I don't have a problem with how you look, but I'm concerned that the extra weight you're carrying around may hurt your health. How about we come up with a plan to make you healthier and feel better about yourself.
7. I'm going grocery shopping. What fruit and veggies do you want me to get? Any other energy snacks you'd like?
8. It sounds like they're making you feel like you're defined by how much you weigh. But you're not. What's more important is that you're <positive attributes: a good friend, funny, caring, creative, etc.>.

9. Let's talk about how you can achieve a weight that is healthier for you and helps you do the things you want to do.
10. Like some of your friends who may have asthma or trouble concentrating, <overweight person's name> carries around too much weight and that can hurt her health too.
11. Most people who don't struggle with their weight have no idea how hard it is to lose weight.
12. That <healthy snack> is a great snack choice. In fact, it looks so good that I think I'll have one too.
13. That looks tasty, but is it good for your body and mind? How does it make you stronger? Let's see if we can find something satisfying that will give you more energy.
14. The more you can work these healthy habits into your daily routine, the healthier you'll be. It also can increase your self-confidence.
15. There are lots of things we can do to become healthier—exercise 20 or more minutes a day, stop drinking soda, have more sit-down family meals, eat more fruits and vegetables, cut out nighttime dessert, etc. What should we try first?
16. Up for a few rounds of <Dance Dance Revolution/Wii Fit/other active video game>?
17. What are your favorite foods? How do you think we can make them healthier?
18. Wow, your hair looks really healthy and shiny. It must be all the fruits and veggies you've been eating lately.
19. Yes, <overweight person> does struggle with carrying extra weight, but that doesn't mean that it is right for anyone to make a comment about how she looks. In fact, I'm sure it hurts her feelings.
20. You heard the doctor say you're gaining weight too quickly. Do you want to talk about what we can do to help you become healthier?
21. You've been practicing <sport/activity> a lot lately and I can definitely see an improvement. What are some things we can do at home to help you get even <stronger/faster/etc.>? Why don't' we see what foods will give you more <strength/stamina/etc.> and I'll work them into our meals.

Did You Know?

Conversations that focus on losing weight and dieting to improve appearance are shown to *increase* the risk for adolescent eating disorders, while focusing on eating well and exercising to improve overall health and energy is preventative. Bottom line: Encourage your teen to embrace healthy habits rather than reach a number on the scale.[23]

Talking Tip

Words to avoid when talking about weight:

- Appearance/looks
- Diet/calories
- Size/fat/thin

Related Tools

- Reliable Resources Cheat Sheet

Related Chapters

- Boost Your Teen's Self-Esteem
- Coax Your Teen to Open Up to You
- Comfort Your Teen
- Encourage Accountability
- Motivate Your Teen
- Tackle Tough Topics
- Body Image
- Being Bullied
- Puberty (Boys)
- Puberty (Girls)
- Tolerance

40 Power Phrases about Peer Pressure

"You have brains in your head. You have feet in your shoes. You can steer yourself any direction you choose. You're on your own. And you know what you know. And YOU are the one who'll decide where to go."—Dr. Seuss

1. Anytime you need an excuse not to do something, feel free to make me the bad guy.
2. Apparently, <behavior> is a growing problem at your school. Is that true? What do you know about it? You know how I feel about it, right? What are your thoughts?
3. Are you ever afraid that you'll lose a friend if you say "no?" Do you believe if someone is truly your friend that they would want you to do something you don't feel comfortable doing?
4. Be sensitive to others, but don't go along with something you don't believe is right—even if others are doing it. You're the only one responsible for how you act.
5. Do you ever worry that you'll be made fun of if you don't go along with the crowd?
6. Do you feel pressure to <behavior> or to act as if you have when you're with friends? How do you handle it?
7. Do your friends make you feel good or bad about yourself?
8. Hanging out with people who like doing similar stuff may help you avoid a situation where you feel pressured into things that you don't want to do. Remember that being seen hanging out with the "cool crowd" might not be as much fun as it looks—especially if you're not comfortable with the decisions that crowd is making.
9. Have a great time tonight. Remember to make smart choices and be true to yourself. I love you.
10. Have you ever seen someone resist peer pressure? What did they do? How did the group react? What did you think about it?
11. Having the strength to say no can be hard, but it also can make you feel good to stick to what you believe in. Explain to people in a calm

way why you don't want to be part of something, and you just might earn respect from others and gain confidence in yourself.

12. How many of your friends or classmates are <behavior>? Does that make you want to do it more? Why? What do you think will happen if you don't? [Note: teens often overestimate the percentage of their peers that are sexually experienced.]
13. I heard that <name> was caught <behavior>. What do you know about that? What do you think about it?
14. I know how hard it is to be in awkward situations. I've found that if you come up with a plan ahead of time it's easier to handle it. Have you thought about what you'll say or do if someone asks you to do something you know is wrong?
15. I know that you spend a lot of time with <name>. I have reason to believe he is <behavior>. Has he ever encouraged you to do that? If yes, what did you do? If no, what would you do if he did?
16. I probably don't understand. Maybe you can help me. What are the pressures around <behavior>.
17. I remember that pit in my stomach that I got when I was your age and the kids I hung out with started doing something that made me feel uncomfortable—for example <share personal story>. Trying to decide if I should go with the flow or say no and risk rejection really stressed me out. I'll tell you, though, I'm most proud of the times that I stuck to my beliefs and said no.
18. I understand how important it is to fit in with your friends. Do you think it's more important than being true to yourself?
19. If you asked your friend to do something and she said no, how would you react?
20. If your friend continues to pressure you into doing something after you've already said no, he is not a true friend and does not have your best interest in mind. A true friend will respect your decision.
21. Imagine your friends are pressuring you to <behavior>, what would you do?

22. It is tough to be the only one who says no to peer pressure, but you can do it. Paying attention to your own feelings and beliefs can help you determine what the right thing is to do. I know I believe in you.
23. It seems like you've been hanging out with a new group of kids lately. Is something up with your old friends, or are you just branching out and meeting some new kids? Tell me about your new friends. What are they like? What do they like to do? What do you like about them?
24. It's hard to stand up for what you believe when everyone else is pushing something different. It's even hard for adults. So how do you resist peer pressure?
25. Just say, "No thanks." Stand up straight and make eye contact. This sends the message that you really mean it.
26. Listen to your gut. Even if your friends seem to be OK with what's going on, if you feel uncomfortable, it means that something about the situation is wrong for you.
27. No one has the right to pressure you into doing something that makes you uncomfortable. <Behavior> is too big a deal to be based on what other people do or say.
28. Peer pressure comes in many different forms. You might feel it in group situations, or you might have friends who try to get you to do things that make you uneasy, like smoke cigarettes, drink, cheat on a test, or skip school. What ideas do you have for staying true to yourself?
29. People are saying that a lot of kids at your school are <behavior>. Are you aware of this? What do you and your friends think about it? Do I need to review why I hope you don't <behavior>?
30. True friends will respect your mind, your rights, and your independent choices.
31. What do you think a "frenemy" is? Do you have any frenemies? How do you handle them? Why do you still hang out with them?
32. What does peer pressure mean to you? What is a good example of peer pressure?

33. What's the worst thing that could happen if you say no to your friends?
34. When you feel like you have to act or dress a certain way because everyone else is doing it, that's called "unspoken pressure." It's OK to follow a trend, but being yourself is cool too.
35. Who are the most popular kids at your school? Do you want to be part of that group? Is there anything that you would/wouldn't do to have them accept you?
36. Who are the people you respect more: The ones who give in and go with the crowd or the ones who stand up for themselves and say no? Which one would you prefer to be?
37. Why do you think people give into peer pressure and do things they don't want to do? What would you tell them to do instead?
38. Why do you think people try to pressure others into doing things that they don't want to do? What do those people get out of it?
39. You know, you'll probably have to make some really tough decisions when you're with those friends. But I guess you're confident in making those decisions, right? If not, you're OK accepting the consequences, whatever they might be, yes?
40. You might be surprised by how many of your friends feel the same way you do.

Did You Know?

"The stress of resisting unhealthy peer pressure can be buffered by good family relationships and a high self-esteem, and it is often those adolescents with neither who succumb to unhealthy pressure from their peers." —L. Eugene Arnold, *Childhood Stress*

Talking Tip

Role-play with your teen so that he feels comfortable and confident when confronted with real peer pressure situations. Try practicing the following statements with him:

- I don't think we should do this.
- I feel really weird about this.
- I'll pass.
- My parents said I have to be home by …
- My parents will kill me if they find out.
- No, thank you.
- Thanks for asking, but no.
- This makes me uncomfortable.

Related Chapters

- Boost Your Teen's Self-Esteem
- Coax Your Teen to Open Up to You
- Encourage Accountability
- Prompt Your Teen to Problem-Solve
- Tackle Tough Topics
- Appearance
- Popularity
- Stress/Pressure to Succeed

25 Power Phrases about Popularity

"He liked to like people, therefore people liked him." —Mark Twain

1. Are there a lot of different cliques at your school? What are they? What do you think about them? Are you a part of any of them?
2. Being popular often comes at a big price. Popular kids are often terrified of losing their status and feel the need to do things that they don't want to do to maintain it. They no longer have the freedom to be true to themselves because they have to conform to fit in.
3. Do you think it's more important to be cool or kind? Is it possible to be both? Do you know anyone who is?
4. Has anyone at your school gone from being popular to a "no one"? How about the other way? What happened?
5. How do you describe popularity? How is that different from being well-liked?
6. How do you think your classmates would describe you? What group are you considered a part of?
7. How do you think your life would be different if you were/weren't part of the "in crowd"?
8. How would being popular make you happier? What is the main reason that you want to part of the "in crowd"?
9. I remember that being popular was really important in high school, but it was so long ago for me that I forgot why. Remind me.
10. I'm so glad that I'm an adult and don't have to worry about being popular anymore. How do you handle it?
11. Is it more important to be popular or to be passionate about something?
12. Is there anything you can't do now that you could do if you were part of the "in crowd"?
13. TV and movies can make it seem like girls need to be sexy to be popular. But your body deserves to be treated with respect, and you deserve to be valued for who you are.

14. Want to know the real secret to being popular and having friends? Be a good friend yourself. Be the kind of friend you'd like to have and stay true to who you are.
15. What do you have in common with the popular kids? Do they have the same interests as you?
16. What does being popular mean to you? Being liked? Respected? Admired? Feared?
17. What famous people do you most admire? What do you admire about them? Let's go online and see if they were popular at your age.
18. What type of reputation do the kids in the "in crowd" have? Is that the reputation you want?
19. What would you be willing to do to be accepted into the "in crowd"? Change your style of dress or hair? Break curfew? Drink? Drive recklessly? Smoke? Take drugs? Shoplift? Have sex? Is it worth it?
20. What would you be willing to give up to be popular? Friends? Activity?
21. What would you do if the group insisted that you act mean to other kids or do something you don't want to do?
22. What/who determines who is popular and who's not?
23. Who are the popular kids at your school? What makes them popular?
24. Why is it so important to you to be popular?
25. Would you rather have a few friends that like you for who you are or a lot of people look up to you because of who they think you are?

Did You Know?

Acceptance by a specific peer group and how good teens feel about themselves and their own achievements are more important to their social development and self-esteem than popularity.

Talking Tip

Teach your teen how to make (and keep) friends:

1. Be nice to everyone. A simple "hi" and genuine compliment go a long way.

2. Don't try too hard. Relax and be yourself.
3. Exude confidence. Stand up straight. Look people in the eye.
4. Join a club or activity you love.
5. Show interest in others. Listen and ask questions.
6. Smile and laugh. People are drawn to happy, positive people.
7. Stay well groomed. At least shower and brush your hair!
8. Take it slowly. Beware of becoming clingy.

Related Chapters

- Challenge a Sense of Entitlement
- Tackle Tough Topics
- Appearance
- Body Image
- Bullying Others
- Dating
- Peer Pressure
- Shyness/Insecurity

16 Power Phrases about Pornography

"Most of the people who join the porn industry come from broken homes. Many of the girls are sexually abused. So the porn industry actually lures in these kind of people to exploit them."—Shelley Lubben, Ex-Porn Star

1. How many times do you think you've looked for these kinds of pictures or videos online? Would you say you've been looking at this stuff for the last month or longer than that? How many times have you seen it in the last week or two?
2. I found evidence that someone in our home has been looking at inappropriate sites online. Once I get to the bottom of it, we can put some precautions in place. Until then, just understand that I'm restricting access to certain kinds of online material. Don't worry: You can still get to some of your favorite websites.
3. I get why you may be interested in porn, but I want you to realize that porn teaches you to see the opposite sex as a thing to be used rather than a person to be loved. I want more for you than that.
4. I know that watching images like this can really stir your sexual desires. I should have talked to you more about these kinds of desires before this. I apologize. Do you have any questions for me?
5. I noticed that you were searching for <search term>. What made you curious about that? Did you find anything <interesting/surprising/confusing>?
6. I want to talk to you about some of the websites/magazines you've been looking at. How did you find them? Why have you been looking at these?
7. I want you to understand why I'm concerned about you looking at pornography. Do you think it portrays sex in a realistic way? Is it respectful to women?
8. I'm not upset about your curiosity, but I do want to know what you've been looking at. Can you bring up the last site you were

on? Do you have any questions about what you saw? If you are uncomfortable showing me, why?

9. If you are curious about sex, there are better ways to learn about it. You can ask me anything. If you aren't comfortable doing that, I'll help you find another reliable resource to answer your questions.
10. If you see any images online that make you uncomfortable or you find confusing, you can always come to me. I want to hear your questions. I don't want you to get answers from disreputable sources.
11. It is quite normal to be curious about the human body, but getting answers from <online/TV/magazine> can be very misleading. I'm happy to talk to you anytime if you have questions about our bodies and sex.
12. My knee-jerk response is to put more parental controls on the computer or ban you from it altogether, but I don't want to do that. I'd rather have you learn how to make responsible choices and protect yourself when you're online. How can I help you do that? What can you do to show me that you're mature enough to handle yourself online?
13. Porn is very deceiving. Often, men and women in porn don't like the work they do. They have to take drugs and alcohol just to be able to have sex on screen. Many of the women were abused when they were young, and they continue to be used and abused in the porn industry. It turns something that should be beautiful and loving into something ugly and abusive.
14. The people in porn are all playing a part. They are actors and actresses in a movie. Then the films are edited to take out all the boring parts and make the actors look their best. It's not reality. It can warp your expectations and take away your enjoyment of sex in the future.
15. There are naked pictures and videos all over the Internet, and I probably should have talked to you about them before today. I am sorry I didn't help you with this earlier. But I'm here now. Do you have any questions about what you've seen? I'll do my best to answer them.
16. What you have been watching can be pretty confusing, even scary, and it doesn't represent real life. Do you have any questions about what you've seen?

Did You Know?

Ninety-three percent of boys and 62 percent of girls are exposed to Internet porn before the age of 18. A quarter of them stumbled upon it when they weren't even looking for it. Sixty-nine percent of boys and 23 percent of girls surveyed said that they have spent at least 30 consecutive minutes viewing Internet porn on at least one occasion.[24]

Talking Tip

The main reasons that teens watch porn are:

1. They stumbled upon it accidentally.
2. They're curious.
3. They're lonely.
4. They've developed an addiction.
5. They use it to masturbate.

Related Tools

- Internet Use Agreement

Related Chapters

- Buy More Time to Respond
- Clarify the Facts
- Coax Your Teen to Open Up to You
- Confront a Teen Who's Lying
- Encourage Accountability
- Tackle Tough Topics
- Puberty (Boys)
- Puberty (Girls)
- Sex: Answers to Common Questions
- Technology Use and Safety

18 Power Phrases about Puberty (Boys)

"Other than dying, I think puberty is probably about as rough as it gets." —Rick Springfield

1. A **cracking voice** means your vocal cords are lengthening and thickening. This usually lasts a few months, but you'll come out of it with a deeper voice.
2. As you get older you're going to develop more muscles and testosterone. They'll make you feel stronger, but also more **aggressive**. You'll have to learn to control this new strength, especially around girls and kids smaller than you.
3. During puberty, you'll probably go through a **growth spurt** and grow about four inches a year. Your head, hands, and feet are the first things to grow. Then your arms and legs, and finally your torso and shoulders. With all this quick growth, you may feel clumsy or awkward. This is normal, too. As the rest of your body catches up, you'll feel less klutzy.
4. Every guy grows at a different time, and you may find that you haven't grown very much while all of your friends are suddenly hovering over you. Most guys don't reach their adult heights until their late teens or early 20s, so you still have time to grow. It may just take more time.
5. Every guy's body is different. Some guys will develop thick **body hair** during puberty, while others won't see a major change in their amount of body hair. Some people are just naturally hairier than others.
6. I know it sucks if your friends or peers are developing **muscles** and you're not. Your body is on a different schedule, but it'll get there in time. You can lift weights, but since you haven't quite reached puberty yet, it'll tone your muscles, but it won't make them bigger. You'll get there eventually though. Until then, what other traits can you work on?

7. I've noticed that you don't like to take your shirt off in front of people anymore. Are you comfortable telling me why? I want you to know that many boys develop a **swelling in their chests** when they're around 13-14 years old. This is perfectly natural and does not mean you're developing breasts. It just means that your body is adjusting to its new form. It'll stop in 1 to 2 years.
8. It's very normal to get an erection for no reason at all, especially when you're going through puberty. It can be embarrassing because you can't predict it. There's not much you can do to suppress **spontaneous erections**, although some guys try to think of something "unsexy" to try to make it go away. Usually the only thing you can do is wait for it to go away and know that it'll happen less frequently as you get older.
9. Just because you're **developing later** doesn't mean you can't excel in a sport. Coaches like someone who's quick, accurate, and consistent. Ask your coach if he has any drills or exercises that you can do at home that will improve these skills and help you learn to control your body better.
10. Many boys your age worry that their **penis** is too small. That almost never turns out to be the case. But if you're really concerned about it, we can set up an appointment with our family doctor to make sure.
11. One of the first places that guys begin to **grow hair** is under their arms and above their upper lips. Once you do, you can start shaving. Want me to show you how?
12. One of the first **signs of puberty** is that your testicles begin to increase in size. After that your penis and scrotum will start to grow as well. Then you'll start growing body hair on your armpits, pubic region, arms, legs, chest, face, hands, and feet. Your hair will not only grow in new places, but it may become thick and darker as well.
13. There are actually some pluses to **not starting puberty** just yet. You don't have to shave, and you might not need to shower as often! So try not to dwell on when your body will change. It will eventually, believe me.

14. There is no universal **penis size**. The average adult penis length is around 3.7 inches when it is not erect and 6-7 inches when erect. Sometimes your penis will get smaller, especially in the cold. Testicles don't come in set sizes either—in fact, one may hang lower than the other. This is normal.
15. **Wet dreams** or *nocturnal emissions* happen to all boys during puberty. Sometimes, when you have a wet dream, you can remember having a sexual dream, but many times you may just notice a wet patch on your pajamas, underwear, or sheets when you wake up. This is nothing to be ashamed of or embarrassed by, and they'll stop when you get older. If it happens, just throw your sheets in the wash.
16. When your sweat and oil producing glands start developing, they often get clogged, which causes **acne**. In order to avoid breakouts, you should wash your face twice daily. If you still break out regularly, let me know and we can speak with a dermatologist.
17. Your body has been going through a lot of changes and you're becoming more like a man. Sometimes this is very confusing and frustrating, I know. But remember, there's a purpose to this.
18. Your **height** will probably end up normal for our family whether you go through puberty early, on average, or late. In fact, when your friends and classmates have stopped growing, you'll probably keep going.

Did You Know?

Boys begin puberty later than girls, typically between the ages of 9 and 14.

Talking Tip

Boys are usually more comfortable talking about their bodies with other males. If possible, have your son talk with his dad, uncle, or another trusted male adult.

Related Tools

- Stages of Puberty Cheat Sheet (Boys)

Related Chapters

- Buy More Time to Respond
- Tackle Tough Topics
- Body Image
- Dating
- Hygiene (or Lack Thereof)
- Pornography
- Puberty (Girls)
- Sex: Abstinence
- Sex: Answers to Common Questions
- Sex: Birth Control
- Sex: STDs
- Sex: Starting "The Talk"

14 Power Phrases about Puberty (Girls)

"Going through puberty as a young girl is so confusing. This monster invades your body, changes things and makes things grow, and no one tells you what's going on." —Katharine Isabelle

1. **Breasts** come in all shapes and sizes, there's no such thing as 'normal' breasts. They are beautiful no matter what their size.
2. Despite what you may have heard, you can't make your **breasts** grow faster, and you can't slow down your body's development either. All you can do is remember that everyone evens out in the end.
3. During puberty, a female's ovaries begin to release one ovum each month. Once that process has begun, a female is capable of becoming **pregnant** any time she has vaginal intercourse with a male partner.
4. Every girl develops differently and at her own pace, so don't be discouraged. No matter in what order your body changes happen, just know you're on your way to becoming a woman—and that is an awesome thing!
5. I have a fun idea. Why don't we go shopping. Maybe even try on a **bra** or two. They have some really cute ones at <store name> and they have professional fitters so we can get something you know you'll be comfortable in.
6. It's healthy to gain some **weight** and put on some fat during puberty, especially along your upper arms, thighs, and upper back. Your hips will grow rounder and wider; your waist will become narrower. The best thing you can do is continue to eat healthy foods and exercise.
7. Some of the **changes** in your body are preparing you for sex—although you want to wait until you're emotionally ready for it as well. The changes also mean your body is maturing to be able to create children.
8. Sometimes, vaginal discharge can become white, clumpy, thick or milky. In this case, you might have a **yeast infection**. Talk to me if this happens so I can buy you something to treat it with.

9. There's no reason to be embarrassed about needing a **bra**. It's a normal part of growing up. If you'd rather keep it quiet, though, we can avoid stores with large crowds or where your friends shop.
10. Usually one of the first **signs of puberty** is that your breasts will start to grow. Then you'll start getting hair in places like the pubic area and under your arms. About two years after that, you'll probably get your period. You'll also notice that your hips, thighs and bottom will get rounder as you transform from a girl into a beautiful woman.
11. **Vaginal discharge** is your vagina's way of cleaning itself, and unlike your period, you can get it on any day of your cycle. As long as your discharge is whitish-yellow or clear and has little or no smell, it's no big deal. If your discharge is foul smelling, painful, or greenish-grey, tell me immediately—you might have a vaginal infection.
12. What are some physical changes that you anticipate during your teen years? What are some of your questions or concerns about these changes?
13. Why do you think many girls often become more self-conscious and less confident as they begin to develop? How can you avoid these pitfalls of maturing?
14. Your **breasts** will grow slowly over several years and it's common for one breast to be larger than the other. Don't worry. They will even out as you get older.

Did You Know?

Girls typically begin experiencing the first signs of puberty between the ages of 8 and 12.

Talking Tip

Break up your talks about puberty into several short sessions over a long period of time to give your daughter time to focus on only one thing at a time.

Related Tools

- Stages of Puberty Cheat Sheet (Girls)

Related Chapters

- Buy More Time to Respond
- Tackle Tough Topics
- Body Image
- Dating
- Hygiene
- Puberty (Boys)
- Puberty: Menstruation
- Sex: Abstinence
- Sex: Answers to Common Questions
- Sex: Birth Control
- Sex: Pregnancy
- Sex: STDs
- Sex: Starting "The Talk"

10 Power Phrases about Puberty: Menstruation

"I mean if there was any justice in the world you wouldn't even have to go to school during your period. You'd just stay home for five days and eat chocolate and cry." —Andrea Portes, *Anatomy of a Misfit*

1. It's normal to feel apprehensive about menstruating, but it's nothing to be worried about. Remember, I'm always here to answer your questions.
2. Many girls have cramps for a day or two each month, typically in the lower abdomen or back, when their periods begin. Other signs and symptoms might include bloating, tender breasts, headaches and fatigue. Exercise, warm baths, a heating pad, or an over-the-counter pain reliever can help ease discomfort.
3. No one can tell exactly when a girl will get her first period. However, typically girls begin menstruating when they're about 12 or 13 years old or two to three years after their breasts begin to develop.
4. Premenstrual syndrome (PMS) happens right before you get your period. It may cause mood swings and irritability, tension, bloating, breakouts, back pain, and breast tenderness. Not everyone gets PMS, but if you do, getting plenty of rest, exercise, and eating a balanced diet might help.
5. Some girls have their period for three days and others have it for a week. Periods can be light, moderate, or heavy, and there usually is about two-to four tablespoons of blood. This can vary from period to period.
6. Tampons can be frustrating to use at first, but it'll get easier with a little practice. Because the muscles of the vagina can become tense when you're nervous, it can be difficult to insert a tampon at first. It's important to relax as much as possible. It's a good idea to start with a slim tampon with an applicator because they can be easier to insert. It can also help to first try a tampon on a day with heavier flow, so that it is easier to put in.

7. Toxic shock syndrome (TSS) is a rare but serious bacterial infection that can be associated with tampon use. Fortunately, TSS almost always can be prevented by changing tampons regularly and by using the smallest absorbency needed (for example, "slender regular" instead of "super plus"). A reasonable precaution is to change tampons every four hours or more frequently if your blood flow is heavy.
8. When I was your age, I was really worried about getting my first period because I thought it would hurt a lot. Are you worried about that?
9. You can do everything that you normally do when you're on your period—as long as you're comfortable.
10. Your period or menstrual cycle happens once a month. Your uterus builds up a lining to nourish a baby. If the egg isn't fertilized (which would lead to pregnancy), then your body sheds the lining, which comes out of your vagina. When you have your period, you'll have to use protection because your clothing might get stained with the blood.

Did You Know?

Most girls get their first period between 11 and 13 years old, though it can start anywhere from ages 8 to 16. Most experts recommend teaching your daughter about menstruation before her first period to help her avoid any shock or embarrassment.[25]

Talking Tip

Teens often worry about how much they'll bleed. Generally, it's 1-2 tablespoons to ½ cup. Demonstrate what your daughter can expect using blue food coloring, water, and three pads. Pour 2 tablespoons into one pad, ¼ cup into another and ½ cup into another. Now she has a gauge of what is healthy.

Quick Trick

Prepare a period pack:

Find a small, inconspicuous case that your teen can carry in her school bag or put in her locker. Fill it with emergency products such as: maxi pads, panty liners, tampons, ibuprofen (if allowed by the school), marjoram oil, ginger tea, and a change of underwear.

Related Tools

- Stages of Puberty Cheat Sheet (Girls)

Related Chapters

- Buy More Time to Respond
- Tackle Tough Topics
- Body Image
- Hygiene
- Puberty (Girls)
- Sex: Abstinence
- Sex: Answers to Common Questions
- Sex: Birth Control
- Sex: Pregnancy
- Sex: STDs
- Sex: Starting "The Talk"

16 Power Phrases about Religion/Faith/Spirituality

"Adolescence is an age where the individual is concerned with what is spiritual and sacred." —Samuel Pfromm Netto, *Psychology of Adolescence*

1. Are there any religions that you're curious about? Do you want me to drive you to any services to check them out?
2. Do you want to pray/meditate with me? Is there anything that you'd like me to pray for?
3. How can I help you grow as a <religion>?
4. How do you define spirituality? Do you think it's important?
5. How do you feel about our religion? Is this a faith that you would have chosen for yourself even if you weren't born into it?
6. How do you feel the services have been lately?
7. I understand that you need to figure out for yourself how religion fits into your life. I will do my best to respect that, however I would like to share with you why <religion> is so important to me. Can I do that?
8. I'm going to <church/mosque/synagogue/temple/etc.> tomorrow. I'd love for you to join me if you're interested.
9. My opinion about religion is … How do you feel about religion?
10. Our faith guides us to believe that ... What are your thoughts about that?
11. Our family's religion is important to me because …
12. Ultimately, it's your choice, but I want you to know why it would mean a lot to me if you embraced our religion …
13. What are your religious beliefs?
14. What do you know about our religion? Do you have any questions for me about it?
15. What does it mean to you to be a <religion>? This is what it means to me …
16. What role does faith play in your life?

Did You Know?

Parents (particularly mothers) are key influencers on their teen's religious beliefs. Three out of 4 religious teens consider their own beliefs somewhat or very similar to those of their parents.[26]

Talking Tip

When teens rebel against their family's religion, it's often more about separating themselves from their parents and exploring their individuality than the religion itself. The more you try to force your religion onto your teen, the more he'll push it away. It's more effective to let your teen discover his faith on his own terms. Chances are, he'll come back to the religion that he grew up with.

Related Chapters

- Tolerance

13 Power Phrases about School Violence

"Violence in our schools can never be tolerated. When children pass through the schoolhouse door, they should find safety, not violence." —Elizabeth Dole

1. Do you and your friends feel safe at your school?
2. Have you heard about the school shootings in … this week? How do you feel about it? I want you to know that it is very unlikely that something like that will happen in your school and all the parents and teachers are doing everything that they can to keep you safe.
3. How have they addressed this tragedy at your school?
4. I don't know exactly why this happened, but it makes me worry about ... What do you think caused this?
5. I feel so bad for those students and their families. What about you?
6. I heard that the student who did the shooting was picked on at school. Why do you think he did it?
7. I think what happened is terrifying. How are you feeling about this?
8. Is there anything that I can do to make you feel safer?
9. Is there anything that you feel like doing about this to help you and your classmates heal?
10. What do you think will help you and your classmates feel safe at school again?
11. What have you heard about <headline>? How do you feel about it? Why do you think these things happen?
12. What is the safety plan at your school if something like this ever happens there?
13. What would you do if someone whom you know threatens violence, himself, or others? [Answer: Tell you or a school official.]

Did You Know?

Less than 1 percent of all homicides among school-age children happen on school grounds or on the way to and from school. Most students will never experience violence at school or in college[27]

Talking Tip

Help your teen feel more secure at school:

1. Create an emergency plan with your teen: Include who to call, where to go, etc.
2. Encourage your teen to talk about her concerns and feelings—and validate them.
3. Make school safety a regular table topic.
4. Review the school's safety procedures.
5. Watch for signs of distress: Arguing more, emotional withdrawal, etc.

Related Tools

- Reliable Resources Cheat Sheet

Related Chapters

- Challenge a Sense of Entitlement
- Coax Your Teen to Open Up to You
- Comfort Your Teen
- Tackle Tough Topics
- Being Bullied
- Bullying Others
- Death and Dying
- Depression
- Suicide and Suicidal Thoughts
- Tolerance

22 Power Phrases about Sex: Starting "the Talk"

(Gulp!)

"'Dad? What did Grandpa tell you about sex?' 'He said if I got a girl pregnant, he'd kill me.'" —Steve Herrick, *Slice*

1. Choosing to be in a sexual relationship is a big decision. I want to make sure you fully understand how it will impact you emotionally and are aware of the possible health risks.
2. Do you know the difference between sex and love?
3. Do you think there is a lot of pressure to have sex at your school?
4. Even if you're not sexually active now, it's important to know how to protect yourself for later. I'd like to talk to you about ...
5. Have you talked about sex at school yet? I know it might be awkward, but I'd like to hear what you've learned so far and answer any questions that you might have.
6. Have your friends had "The Talk" with their parents yet? How'd that go?
7. I don't think having sex at your age is a good idea and I hope you choose not to. However, if you're going to have sex, all I ask is that you are responsible and safe. Let's chat a bit about what you need to know.
8. I hear a lot of stories about what kids are doing sexually and it scares me a bit. I want to make sure that you are safe and have all the information that you need to make wise choices.
9. I prefer that you wait to have sex because ... However, when you are 100 percent sure that you are ready and doing it with the right person for the right reasons, I want to know that you are protecting yourself from STDs and pregnancy.
10. I've noticed that you and <boy/girlfriend> have been dating awhile and are really happy together. I don't want to pry, but I'm wondering

if the subject of intimacy and sex has come up. Have you discussed how you are going to handle it and make sure you're safe?

11. If you felt pressured to have sex, how would you handle that? What if you wanted to have sex, but your boy/girlfriend felt pressured by you?
12. Is there someone you really like? What kinds of things do you do together? Have you ever felt pressured or wanted to have sex?
13. It's OK and actually important for you to understand your own body and sexual responses. Although it may be uncomfortable to talk about it, I'd like to try.
14. It's OK to think about sex and to feel sexual desire—most people do. But you want to protect yourself from getting pregnant/getting someone pregnant and STDs. Do you know what you'll do if someone wants to have sex with you?
15. Sex should always be mutually consensual and pleasurable for both people involved. It's not about taking, using, or hurting, but rather respect and caring. How do you show respect toward the person you're with?
16. The female/male body can be pretty confusing to understand. Is there anything that you'd like me to explain?
17. What did you learn in Sex Ed today? Yes, I remember learning that when I was your age. What was your reaction?
18. What do you and your friends think about the Sex Ed classes at school? What information do they cover?
19. What kind of questions do you have about sex? I know it can be awkward to talk about it, but I'd rather you get answers from me than your friends so I know that you're getting accurate and safe information.
20. What would you say to a friend who was considering having sex now?
21. When do you think it's OK to <kiss/make out/have sex/etc.>?
22. You and <boy/girlfriend> have been seeing a lot of each other lately. At your age, I'm sure that a lot of strong feelings come up when you're around each other. I'd like to talk to you about those and make sure that you are prepared to make smart choices.

Did You Know?

Most younger teens are NOT having sex. At age 15, only 16 percent of teens have had sex, and at 17, more than half (52 percent) are still virgins. Repeated surveys show that teens think that more of their peers are sexually active than actually are. And the majority of teens who have had sex wish they had waited longer.[28]

Talking Tip

When talking to your teen about sex, remember to:

1. Be clear about your own sexual values and morals.
2. Encourage open communication.
3. Focus on educating and encouraging your teen to make healthy decisions.
4. Go beyond biology: Talk about feelings, relationships, responsibility, and respect.
5. Make yourself available to answer questions.
6. Provide the facts: Use the correct terms for body parts.
7. Stay calm.
8. Stress safety.
9. Talk, don't preach.
10. Talk with your child early and often about sex and sexuality.

Related Tools

- Reliable Resources Cheat Sheet
- Dating Agreement

Related Chapters

- Grab Your Teen's Attention
- Tackle Tough Topics

- Dating
- Hygiene
- Puberty (Boys)
- Puberty (Girls)
- Puberty: Menstruation
- Sex: Abstinence
- Sex: Answers to Common Questions
- Sex: Birth Control
- Sex: STDs

25 Power Phrases about Sex: Abstinence

"Too often the message ends at abstinence and students are denied the information they need when they do become sexually active." —David Landry

1. Are you considering having sex now because you want to or because you feel pressured by your boy/girlfriend or peers? Remember, you're in charge of your own life and having sex is a very big decision. Don't let anyone pressure you into having sex before you're ready.
2. Are you prepared for the emotions that you might feel afterward?
3. Before you get physically intimate with someone, ask yourself, "Does he really care about me? "Can I really trust him?" and "Can I truly be myself with him?"
4. Being intimately involved and having sex with someone is a big step in a relationship. I hope you will <wait until you are older/ until you are married/until you are in a committed, long-term relationship/your personal value>, but it is your decision. If you're getting pressured and it's not what you want, then say, "No, I really like you, but I'm not ready for sex right now." What else could you say to her?
5. Everyone remembers the first time that they had sex. If it's with the wrong person or for the wrong reasons it can be hurtful or demeaning and you'll wish you could forget it. But if you wait until you feel truly ready and share it with a person you love it can be incredibly beautiful and wonderful. That's the experience I wish for you.
6. Have you seriously considered the consequences of having sex? In addition to the serious physical consequences, such as STDs and pregnancy, having sex with someone takes your relationship to a whole new level emotionally—are you and your boy/girlfriend ready for that? Have you talked about it? If you're not sure that you're ready or you haven't talked about it (or are too embarrassed to), it might be a good idea to wait.

7. How long do the two of you plan to stay together?
8. I believe it's important to wait to have sex until you're <in love/ engaged/married> because …
9. I know you may think everyone is doing it, most teens think their peers are sexually active, but the fact is most people your age are not having sex. In fact, studies show that over 50 percent of high school students are still virgins and the majority of teens who have had sex wish they had waited.
10. I notice you've been spending a lot of time with <boy/girlfriend>. I'm going to be a protective mom/dad for a second and remind you that if you are thinking about sex or she's pressuring you or you're confused, it's OK to wait. You know that, right?
11. I want to make sure you're prepared for the emotional consequences of having sex: like what if he doesn't call or doesn't say hi to you in school, or worse, he tells all his friends. Are you ready to handle that?
12. I want you to appreciate and enjoy a healthy sex life your whole life. If you have sexual experiences that you feel bad or guilty about, it could affect how you feel about sex down the road.
13. I want your first time and every time to be beautiful and amazing, a time when your body is respected and valued, not used and discarded.
14. If you don't respect your partner, or you know she doesn't respect you, chances are you're going to regret being intimate with her.
15. It's normal for teens to have strong sexual feelings, but it doesn't mean that you have to act on them. Sex is very intimate and emotional and should be done only with someone whom you completely trust.
16. My hope for you is that your first time is with someone whom you love and trust, who is going to respect you and care about you and makes you feel good about yourself.
17. Relationships should make you feel appreciated and respected, not pressured or uncomfortable. If your boy/girlfriend truly cares about you, s/he won't pressure you to do something that you aren't ready for. Tell your boy/girlfriend how you feel. If s/he's the right one for you, s/he'll understand.

18. Sex should always be mutually consensual and pleasurable for both people involved. Do you feel like you respect yourself enough to say no if you're not being respected by the other person?
19. The first time you're sexually active you're going to remember it for the rest of your life, so you want to make sure you're going to feel proud of it.
20. Two people can love each other very much without having sex. Can you think of some other ways to show someone you love her?
21. What do you want your first time to be like?
22. Why do you think you're ready to have sex now?
23. Why do you want to take it to the next level now?
24. You can change your mind and say no whenever you want. Just because you agreed to have sex doesn't mean that you have to go through with it.
25. You know that it's never OK to let anyone pressure you or pressure anyone to do anything sexual that they aren't comfortable doing, right?

Did You Know?

Teens say that their parents have the most influence over their decisions about sex. In fact, 7 in 10 teens say that it would be much easier for them to postpone sexual activity and avoid teen pregnancy if they were able to have more open, honest conversations about these topics with their parents.[29]

Talking Tip

Many parents fear that talking about sex will give their teens the impression that they are OK with them being sexually active. This is not the case. Research shows that teens who talk openly with their parents are actually more likely to delay sexual activity and be responsible and safe.[30]

Related Tools

- Reliable Resources Cheat Sheet
- Dating Agreement

Related Chapters

- Encourage Accountability
- Tackle Tough Topics
- Dating
- Peer Pressure
- Puberty (Boys)
- Puberty (Girls)
- Puberty: Menstruation
- Sex: Abstinence
- Sex: Answers to Common Questions
- Sex: Birth Control
- Sex: Pregnancy
- Sex: STDs
- Sex: Starting "The Talk"

23 Power Phrases about Sex: Answers to Common Questions

"Since most parents are reluctant to talk about sex, schools have tried to fill the gap. In America, when we decide to ignore a subject, our favorite form of denial is to teach it incompetently." —Bob Smith

1. **Am I normal?** "Normal" encompasses a broad range of behaviors, desires, body types, and genital shapes and sizes. What are you specifically concerned about?
2. **Can a girl get pregnant before she has her period?** Yes, a girl can get pregnant if she's never had her period. She also can get pregnant the first time that she has sex and if she has sex during her period.
3. **Can you get an STD from a toilet seat?** No. Sexually transmitted diseases can't live outside the body for a long period of time—especially not on a cold, hard surface like a toilet seat. Plus, they aren't present in urine. So the chances of catching one from whoever used the bathroom before you are pretty slim.
4. **Can you get pregnant just by fooling around?** Yes, it's possible to get pregnant when you're fooling around, even though you may not have intercourse. If the semen from the penis gets anywhere near the vagina, the sperm can find their way into the vagina and travel to an egg. Then you might get pregnant.
5. **Can you get pregnant the first time you have sex?** Absolutely! You are just as likely to get pregnant the first time you have sex as any other time.
6. **How can I tell if I'm ready to have sex?** There is no perfect moment when you'll suddenly know you're ready. Some good questions to ask are: "Am I doing this because I want to, not because I feel pressured?" "Have I seriously considered the consequences of having sex (emotional, pregnancy, STDs)?" "Are my partner and I prepared with two forms of birth control?" "Is my boy/girlfriend also ready to have sex?"

7. **How do I know if I'm doing it right?** Your first time, you probably won't know what you are doing or if you are doing it "right." Try not to worry too much about it. If you are ready, you care about the person whom you're with, and it's consensual, you will enjoy yourself.
8. **How do you get pregnant?** For a girl to get pregnant, the guy's sperm has to get into her vagina. This happens when a boy ejaculates inside a female's vagina or near its opening. His sperm then swim up into the female's Fallopian tubes. If there is an ovum in the Fallopian tube, conception occurs when the sperm fertilizes the egg.
9. **Is oral sex a big deal?** You may think I'm a prude, but to me oral sex is a very intimate, personal act and shouldn't be taken lightly. You can't get pregnant through oral sex, but you can get many different sexually transmitted diseases. Oral sex also can impact you quite a bit emotionally. I can't help but wonder if some of the kids who do it "for fun" actually feel bad about it afterward and wish they hadn't. How do you think it makes them feel?
10. **Is sex painful?** The first time you have sex can be painful for some women. That's because they may have a hymen in the opening of their vaginas that gets stretched open during first intercourse and may cause pain and bleeding.
11. **What is a hickey?** A hickey is made when your partner puts her mouth on your neck and sucks so hard that it leaves a long-lasting mark.
12. **What is a virgin?** A virgin is someone who has never had sexual intercourse.
13. **What is an erection?** A guy has an erection when blood flows into his penis causing it to harden and lengthen. This can happen when he has romantic or sexual thoughts, or when his penis is stimulated. Erections also can happen without any stimulation or romantic thoughts at all, which can be a bit embarrassing if he's in public.
14. **What is an orgasm?** An orgasm is an intense, pleasurable physical feeling that can occur during sex or masturbation. There's a feeling

of buildup and a release, sort of like when you sneeze. During an orgasm, sperm comes out of a man's penis, which is called ejaculation.

15. **What is bisexual?** Bisexual refers to people who are attracted to both men and women.
16. **What is circumcision** OR **why does my penis look different from the other guys?** Male circumcision is the surgical removal of the foreskin from the penis. It is an ancient practice that has its origin in religious rites. Today, many parents have their sons circumcised for religious or health reasons. We decided to have you/not have you circumcised because …
17. **What is French kissing?** A kiss that includes putting your tongues into each other's mouth.
18. **What is homosexuality?** Homosexuality is being sexually and romantically attracted to people of the same sex. Most experts believe that people have no more choice about being homosexual than heterosexual. "Gay" and "lesbian" are used to refer to homosexual men and women.
19. **What is masturbation?** Masturbation is when people touch their own genitals to feel pleasure. It can be a safe, natural way to relieve strong sexual feelings and is nothing to be ashamed of. It is a personal experience that should be done in a private place. There is a lot of misinformation out there, though, so if you have concerns or questions about it, you can talk to me.
20. **What is oral sex?** Oral sex is a very intimate behavior between two people. One person puts their mouth on the other person's genitals to cause sexual pleasure. Although you can't get pregnant through oral sex, it does count as sex and you can get STDs like gonorrhea, herpes, and HIV, so it's very important to always use a condom.
21. **What is rape?** Any form of forced sex is rape, even if it's with someone whom you're dating. What do you do if a girl says no to your advances? Is there ever a time that you should ignore her when she says no? The answer is no. No always means no.
22. **What is the clitoris?** The clitoris is part of the female anatomy that has a lot of nerve endings, which makes it very sensitive.

23. **What is the G-spot?** The G-spot, named after the German gynecologist Ernst Gräfenberg, is a sensitive area of the anterior wall of the vagina believed to be a highly erogenous area. Some people believe it exists, some don't.

Did You Know?

There are many trusted websites that can help you find the answers that you need, including:

- Go Ask Alice: http://goaskalice.columbia.edu
- Teens WebMD: http://teens.webmd.com
- TeensHealth: http://kidshealth.org/teen/
- Teenwire.org: http://teenwire.org
- The Center for Young Women's Health: http://youngwomenshealth.org

Talking Tip

If your teen's questions make you feel embarrassed or uncomfortable, say so. Acknowledging your own discomfort allows your teen to acknowledge his and may even help you both feel a little less awkward.

Related Tools

- Reliable Resources Cheat Sheet

Related Chapters

- Buy More Time to Respond
- Tackle Tough Topics
- Dating
- Homosexuality (Am I Gay?)
- Homosexuality (Coming Out)
- Hygiene

- Puberty (Boys)
- Puberty (Girls)
- Puberty: Menstruation
- Sex: Birth Control
- Sex: Pregnancy
- Sex: STDs
- Sex: Starting “The Talk”

16 Power Phrases about Sex: Birth Control

"We want far better reasons for having children than not knowing how to prevent them." —Dora Winifred Black Russell

1. <Son/Daughter>, here's a condom. I'm not giving this to you because I approve of you having sex at your age—I don't. I love you and think you deserve to have your first time and every time be a loving experience. But I know that you're going to do what you want, and keeping you safe from STDs and pregnancy is extremely important. So keep this on you to remind you to make good choices.
2. Different methods of birth control are better for different people, so it's important to learn about each method before you choose the one that's best for you. Do you want to me to explain any to you?
3. The first time and every time that you have sex there's a chance that you can <get pregnant/get someone pregnant>. The only 100 percent foolproof way to avoid pregnancy is to not have sex in the first place. If you are having sex, it's important that you use protection every single time. No exceptions.
4. Have you and your boy/girlfriend talked about condoms and other forms of birth control?
5. Have you and your boy/girlfriend talked about what happens if you guys get pregnant?
6. If you ever choose to make a different choice about having sex, I hope the two of you will talk it over first, make a careful decision, and see a physician about contraception.
7. If you feel close enough with someone to have sex, you should feel close enough to discuss the need for birth control. Are you ready to do that?
8. If you're not sure how to use your birth control, please let me know. I can explain it or make a doctor's appointment for you if that makes you more comfortable. It's worth a little embarrassment to avoid serious problems.

9. It's really important to use birth control if you're thinking about having sex. Are you prepared with any?
10. Remember, if you're having sex and not using birth control, you're *planning* to get pregnant. You need to talk to your boy/girlfriend about this before you have sex, so you're both comfortable with what you're going to use.
11. Think carefully about your birth control choice. Think about questions like how likely you are to use it every time, how likely you are to use it correctly, and how well it works.
12. To be safe, and because condoms sometimes break, you should always have a second form of birth control. Are you prepared with two forms of birth control?
13. What would you do if you are with someone and they don't want to use a condom? What if they tell you that it doesn't feel as good or that if you use other birth control, condoms aren't necessary? How would you respond?
14. When people decide to have sex, a condom is placed over the penis to prevent pregnancy and sexually transmitted diseases. What else would you like to know about condoms?
15. You know that I prefer that you wait, but it's even more important to me that you are safe. Always carry a condom with you. You can't depend on your partner being prepared.
16. You know that you can get pregnant anytime you have sexual intercourse. Wearing a latex condom, taking birth control pills, or using other contraceptives are very effective at preventing pregnancy. However, the only absolute way to not get pregnant is to not have sex at all. What are you prepared to use?

Did You Know?

Seventy-eight percent of girls who have had intercourse have not used condoms and 56 percent say that they didn't use any birth control at all.[31]

Talking Tip

If left to their own devices, teens hear (and believe) some of the craziest birth-control myths. Make sure to debunk these before your teen resorts to using one:

1. Hot tubs kill sperm, prevent pregnancy, and ward off STDs.
2. If you don't have a condom, use plastic wrap.
3. If you douche with soda after intercourse, you won't get pregnant.
4. If you pee immediately after sex, you won't get pregnant.
5. Mountain Dew lowers your sperm count and can be used as a contraceptive.
6. There is only one day of the month when you can get pregnant.
7. Two condoms are better than one.
8. You don't get pregnant your first time.
9. You're less likely to get pregnant if you jump up and down after sex.

Related Tools

- Reliable Resources Cheat Sheet
- Birth Control Cheat Sheet
- Dating Agreement

Related Chapters

- Encourage Accountability
- Grab Your Teen's Attention
- Tackle Tough Topics
- Dating and Relationships
- Peer Pressure
- Puberty: Menstruation
- Sex: Abstinence
- Sex: Answers to Common Questions
- Sex: Pregnancy
- Sex: STDs
- Sex: Starting "The Talk"

14 Power Phrases about Sex: Pregnancy

"Pregnant teenage girls do not need lectures about 'carelessness', 'stupidity' or 'disregard for family rules or values.' I have witnessed a lot of this type of shaming from parents, and it makes things worse." —Dr. John Duffy

1. Have you and the <mother/father> thought about what you want to do? Ultimately, the decision is <yours/the mother's>, but we can research all the options (having it, adoption, abortion) together so we have all the facts.
2. I'm feeling pretty <emotion>, but I know berating you or freaking out isn't going to resolve anything. Let me take some time to calm down and then I want to talk about what you're feeling and start figuring out what we're going to do.
3. If you decide to keep the baby, you need to understand that, although having a baby can be rewarding, it isn't always fun. Caring for a baby is a huge responsibility and a lifelong commitment. You won't have as much time (if any time) for the things you used to do, like … The baby will always have to take priority. Are you ready for that big of a commitment?
4. Instead of strengthening a relationship or leading to marriage, having a baby often leads to a lot of problems. In fact, most fathers never marry the teen mothers of their babies.
5. It's important that you make sure you keep yourself healthy so that your baby stays healthy. This means eating right, getting enough sleep, keeping caffeine to a minimum and stopping all drinking, smoking, and drugs, if you were doing any of those. Unsafe sex also can be dangerous for the baby. I know it's a lot, but I'm here to help you manage it all. Do you have any questions?
6. Most teen moms say that they love their children but wish they'd waited 10 years to have them. Babies are wonderful, but they need and deserve adult parents who are willing and able to do the demanding and lifelong work of raising a child.

7. Raising a child is hard. Raising a child alone is even harder. Being a teenager is a great time for growing up, getting an education, meeting new people, and having fun—not pregnancy and parenthood.
8. So you're saying I might be a grandparent? It's going to take me some time to adjust to that. How are you feeling about possibly being a <mother/father>?
9. Son, thank you for telling me. How are you feeling about it? You realize that the pregnancy is your responsibility too. Do you love the mom? Are you planning on staying together? Have you discussed what you want to do? How can I help?
10. Thank you for telling me. I imagine this must be the scariest thing you've ever had to deal with and it's not something that you should face alone. I'll help you through this. The first thing we need to do is get you to a doctor to determine how far along you are in your pregnancy and find out what your options are.
11. This question may be a little awkward, but I need to ask. Are you 100 percent sure <who the father is/you're the father>? How much <does he/do you> want to be involved?
12. What do you think about teen pregnancy? How would becoming a parent now change your goals for the future?
13. Wow! I can't deny that I'm <emotion>. I'll need some time to process. But I do want you to know that I love you very much, I'm here for you, and we'll figure this out together.
14. You can still have a future as a young mother, but it'll be different than what either of us had planned for you. Are you willing to make that sacrifice?

Did You Know?

The most important thing parents can do to prevent teen pregnancy is to be involved in their teen's lives.[32]

Talking Tip

Many teens avoid telling their parents that they're pregnant (or got someone pregnant) because they fear their anger and disappointment. Without parental support, teens are less likely to receive adequate prenatal care—which puts them and their babies at risk. With this in mind, the best way to help your pregnant teen is to:

1. Accept and support her. (That doesn't mean you have to be happy about the situation.)
2. Avoid making threats or forcing your opinion on him. (It'll almost always backfire!)
3. Decide how involved you are going to be. (What will you pay for? Will they live with you? Will you help care for the baby?)
4. Find local support groups and services.
5. Get her to a doctor ASAP.
6. Recognize and work through your own feelings.
7. Talk about her options and support her decision.

Related Tools

- Reliable Resources Cheat Sheet
- Birth Control Cheat Sheet

Related Chapters

- Buy More Time to Respond
- Clarify the Facts
- Cool Down a Heated Situation
- Encourage Accountability
- Grab Your Teen's Attention
- Tackle Tough Topics
- Dating and Relationships
- Puberty (Boys)

- Puberty (Girls)
- Puberty: Menstruation
- Sex: Abstinence
- Sex: Birth Control

15 Power Phrases about Sex: STDs

"One of the great misconceptions is that people who have STDs know they have them.... That is absolutely incorrect."—Edward Hook, M.D.

1. Abstinence—not having sex—is the only 100 percent sure way to not get an STD.
2. Are both of you absolutely sure that neither one of you has been with anyone else sexually in any way?
3. Are you and your boy/girlfriend exclusive? Do you know the dangers if you're not?
4. Condoms can't protect you from all STDs. But, if used correctly and used all the time, latex condoms will lower your chances of getting some STDs and getting pregnant. Are you using condoms every single time? Are you confident that you're using them correctly?
5. Do you know that although you can't get pregnant from oral or anal sex, you can still get STDs like herpes and HIV? Do you want help or advice in obtaining protection?
6. What do you know about sexually transmitted diseases?
7. Have you and your boy/girlfriend both been tested for STDs?
8. If two people have sexual intercourse, and one of them has HIV or another STD, she could give it to her partner. Doctors believe that if the man wears a latex condom whenever he has intercourse, it helps to protect him and his partner from giving each other HIV. That's why people call sexual intercourse with a latex condom "safe sex."
9. If you're going to have sex, you have to protect yourself against pregnancy and STDs. At the very least, that means using a condom. Are you comfortable talking about that with your boy/girlfriend? Do you want to practice what you'll say? If not with me, do you have a friend who you can practice with?
10. Just because your partner doesn't show any signs or symptoms, that doesn't mean he's STD-free. The only way to know that you have

an STD is to get tested. Always ask your boy/girlfriend to get tested before engaging in sex and put both your minds at ease.

11. People from all walks of life can (and do) get infected with STDs. STDs don't care if you're promiscuous or a virgin, straight or gay, male or female, old or young — anyone who engages in any type of sexual activity (not just intercourse) is at risk.
12. Some STDs don't show symptoms right away and some require a medical professional to identify them. It's important that you know the signs and symptoms of STDs and protect yourself. I don't know a whole lot about STDs. Let's go on the Internet and get some information.
13. The only sure way to know if you've been infected with an STD is to get tested. Many STDs develop slowly and have little, or no, symptoms. If left untreated, STDs can lead to significant health problems. So tell me, or another adult you trust, immediately if you see something weird or start feeling sick.
14. You can get an STD from both giving and receiving unprotected oral sex—especially if you or your partner has an open sore or your gums bleed. Using a condom or dental dam can help protect you and your partner from STDs, but neither is 100 percent effective.
15. You can get some STDs from skin-to-skin or mouth-to-mouth contact. Kissing can spread herpes. Rubbing your bodies together can pass infections such as genital warts, herpes, scabies, and pubic lice.

Did You Know?

About 1 in 4 sexually active teens (approximately 3 million) gets an STD every year.[33]

Talking Tip

11 Crazy Myths about STDs that Many Teens Believe

1. I can get an STD from a toilet seat.
2. I can only get herpes if my partner is having an outbreak.
3. I can only get the same STD once.
4. I can't get an STD if I only have sex once.
5. I can't get an STD from oral or anal sex.
6. I can't get an STD if I only sleep with virgins.
7. I can't get STDs from skin-to-skin contact.
8. If my partner or I have an STD, we'll know it.
9. Only guys and girls that sleep around get STDs.
10. The chlorine in a pool or hot tub kills STDs.
11. The Pill prevents STDs.

Related Tools

- Reliable Resources Cheat Sheet
- Birth Control Cheat Sheet
- STDs Cheat Sheet

Related Chapters

- Encourage Accountability
- Grab Your Teen's Attention
- Tackle Tough Topics
- Homosexuality (Coming Out)
- Peer Pressure
- Sex: Abstinence
- Sex: Answers to Common Questions
- Sex: Birth Control

10 Power Phrases about Shoplifting/Stealing

"Win a FREE ride in a police car just by shoplifting from this store. Lucky winners will also get their name in the newspaper for their friends and family to see! Won't mom and dad be proud?" —Store sign

1. Do you realize how wrong stealing is? Can you tell me why you thought it was OK for you to take this?
2. Do you understand why stealing is a serious offense? How can you make amends for this poor decision?
3. I am very disappointed in you right now. Try to help me understand why you thought it was OK to steal?
4. I love you and I'll be here for you, but I'm not going to bail you out of this. You made a bad choice and now you have to live with the legal consequences of that, whatever those may be.
5. I want to give you more freedom, but that also means more responsibility. Can I count on you to do the right thing and to behave in a way that is honest and doesn't hurt other people?
6. I want to trust you, but I seriously question your judgment right now. What would you do if you were me right now?
7. Is that new? Where did you get it? How much was it? Where did you get the money?
8. Taking items from a store without paying for them is called shoplifting. It's a crime. If you get caught you could be fined, given a record, and even put in jail.
9. You did something legally and ethically wrong, but I want to give you the chance to make it right. How do plan on doing that?
10. You realize that you need to take that back immediately and deal with whatever the consequences are, right? Do you want me to go with you?

Did You Know?

Shoplifting is an equal-opportunity crime: Boys and girls steal in the same numbers, and every economic and social group is affected.[34]

Talking Tip

Teens shoplift because they're:

- Acting out
- Bored
- Craving attention
- Feeling pressured by their peers
- Seeking a thrill
- Trying to get something they want but can't afford

Related Tools

- Behavior Agreement

Related Chapters

- Buy More Time to Respond
- Challenge a Sense of Entitlement
- Clarify the Facts
- Confront a Teen Who's Lying
- Cool Down a Heated Situation
- Encourage Accountability
- Grab Your Teen's Attention
- Tackle Tough Topics
- Money
- Peer Pressure

18 Power Phrases about Shyness/Insecurity

"I was shy, withdrawn and I didn't have any self-esteem. The year that I was 17 was one of the worst of my life, because I was searching for my place in the world. I was obsessed with a girl for years but I never talked to her because I was extremely shy." —Robert Pattinson

1. Are you afraid you'll embarrass yourself or say something that others might consider stupid? What do you think might happen if you did? How would you react? Are there other ways you could handle it?
2. Are you worried that your peers might ignore you if you try to reach out to them? What could you do if they did?
3. Close your eyes and visualize a situation in which you might be shy. Now reimagine the situation, but with you feeling confident. What did you do differently?
4. Do you ever worry that you'll get tongue-tied and not know what to say if you try to talk to certain people? One way to save yourself in that situation is to ask a question. We could come up with some good questions that you could use in a pinch.
5. Does drawing attention to yourself make you uncomfortable? Why? What's the worst thing that could happen?
6. Everyone—including you—has some special gift or trait to offer to the world. It may sound corny, but it's true. Instead of fixating on the things that make you feel inferior, think of the amazing things that you have to offer, such as ... Then you'll realize that you have plenty to offer any group or situation and feel more comfortable speaking up.
7. How do you feel when you walk into a room? Do you see it as an opportunity, or do you feel like everyone's looking at you critically?
8. How would you choose to act in social situations if you weren't feeling shy or afraid?
9. I know it's tough, but try not to compare yourself to others. It'll only make you feel more intimidated. And the thing is, you have no idea

how they are really feeling inside. Most people are struggling with self-esteem issues and don't feel as confident as you think they do. They've just gotten better at faking it. The more you practice, the better you'll get too. And the better you get at it, the more you'll believe it.

10. Most people become shy because they're afraid they'll embarrass themselves if they speak up. That's why it's important to focus on other people instead. The easiest way to do this is to concentrate on making other people comfortable. If you're concerned about how other people feel, you'll be less concerned about how they see you.
11. One of the biggest things that keep people from achieving their goals—and feeling good about themselves—is negative self-talk. In other words, telling yourself that you're a loser or a failure. Do you ever do this?
12. Some kids are just naturally shy. There isn't anything wrong with that, unless it's preventing you from making friends, participating in classroom discussions, and doing the activities you really enjoy. Do you feel that being shy is preventing you from doing the things that make you happy?
13. There are actually a lot of strengths that come from being shy. Shy people are often better listeners and more sensitive to other people's feelings and emotions. Both are characteristics that most people really value in a friend.
14. Think of the people whom you would want to approach. How do they hold themselves? What are their facial expressions like? Now think of the people whom you wouldn't want to approach. What is their body language like? How does your typical body language compare?
15. Try standing tall. This gives the world the impression that you are self-confident and friendly, and we're usually treated the way we feel (or look like we're feeling). It may even trick your brain into believing it too.

16. What social situations make you the most uncomfortable? Do you want to brainstorm some ways that can help you feel more relaxed or confident in those situations?
17. When people are shy, they often avoid making eye contact with people. But that's often perceived as being stuck up or unfriendly instead of being shy. What's the worst thing that could happen if you look at people and smile? Are there any particular people at school whom you feel comfortable talking to?
18. You can't be comfortable around other people unless you're comfortable being yourself first. What makes you feel uncomfortable around other people?

Did You Know?

Several celebrities have been identified as overcoming shyness. It might help your teen embrace their own shyness if they can find someone to relate to whom they admire: Abraham Lincoln, Albert Einstein, Bill Gates, Blake Lively, Brad Pitt, Carrie Underwood, Eleanor Roosevelt, Elvis Presley, J.K. Rowling, Jim Carrey, Johnny Depp, Kim Kardashian, Kristin Stewart, Lady Gaga, Mia Hamm, Robert Pattinson, Steven Spielberg, Tina Fey, Tom Cruise, and Tom Hanks.

Talking Tip

If you have a shy teen, make an effort to:

1. Help build your teen's self-worth
2. *Not* compare personalities (It's OK to be shy.)
3. *Not* urge your teen to change
4. *Not* try to be your teen's social director
5. Praise your teen's strengths

Related Chapters

- Boost Your Teen's Self-Esteem
- Coax Your Teen to Open Up to You
- Make Your Teen Feel Valued
- Tackle Tough Topics
- Body Image
- Peer Pressure
- Popularity

17 Power Phrases about Stress/Pressure to Succeed

"As stress builds up I begin to cry. I hide. Not my body, but my mind. I can no longer think of anything I used to think about. I can no longer feel what I used to feel. Things seem unreal. Life. Stress. I feel stress." —Kellie Briscoe, *I Feel Stress*

1. Although just enough stress can be a good thing, stress overload can be unhealthy. For example, feeling a little stress about a test that's coming up can motivate you to study hard. But stressing out too much over the test can make it hard to concentrate on the material that you need to learn. Let's talk about ways that you can manage your stress.
2. Although you can't always control the things that are stressing you out, you can control how you react to them. If you change how you think, you can change the way you feel.
3. Don't try to be perfect—no one is. If you need help on something, like schoolwork, ask for it.
4. I want to support and encourage you to do the best you can, but I don't expect you to be perfect. I'm sorry if I've made you feel that way.
5. If you feel like you're being stretched too thin, consider cutting out an activity or two. Which ones are most important to you? Which ones do you think you could live without?
6. It's OK not to be perfect—everyone messes up from time to time. Forgive yourself, remind yourself of all your great accomplishments, and move on.
7. Let's make a list of the things that are causing your stress, including your friends, family, school, and other activities. Is there anything on this list that you can cut out of your life or gain better control of?
8. Putting too much pressure on yourself to do well (like getting good grades) can make you feel bad about yourself. When that happens, it's easy to think there's nothing you can do to change things. But

there is. Let's come up with some ways to manage the pressure that you feel.

9. Remember that you can't make everyone in your life happy all the time. Focus on what makes YOU happy instead.
10. Stress and worry can take a big toll, even leading to depression. If you're feeling stressed-out, please come talk to me or someone else whom you trust.
11. There are safe and unsafe ways to deal with stress. Using drugs or alcohol may seem like tempting ways to escape your problems, but they actually add more problems to stress out about, like addiction, or family and health problems.
12. What do you think my expectations are for you? Do you feel like I put too much pressure on you?
13. What do you think will happen if you don't do this perfectly?
14. What's the worst thing that could happen if you don't succeed at ...?
15. Why do you feel so much pressure to succeed at …?
16. With all the things that happen at your age, it's easy to feel overwhelmed. Things that you can't control are often the most frustrating. Are you feeling overwhelmed or frustrated?
17. You may find yourself feeling anxious about things that didn't matter to you so much before. Anxiety can feel uncomfortable, but it's a sign that you really care about something.

Did You Know?

When parents set high expectations and focus excessively on success and achievements (instead of effort), teens feel pressured to be perfect. Anything short of perfection is perceived as failure. When this perceived failure extends across several aspects of the teen's life (school, relationships, activities), s/he often becomes anxious, depressed, and even suicidal.[35]

Talking Tip

Your teen may be doing too much if she:

1. Constantly feels overwhelmed
2. Doesn't have time for a social life
3. Freaks out if things aren't done "perfectly"
4. Frequently stays up late to finish homework
5. Has a busier schedule than you do

Related Tools

- Homework Agreement

Related Chapters

- Boost Your Teen's Self-Esteem
- Coax Your Teen to Open Up to You
- Comfort Your Teen
- Give Constructive Feedback
- Prevent Misunderstandings
- Prompt Your Teen to Problem-Solve
- Say "I'm Sorry" with Conviction
- Spark Collaboration
- Tackle Tough Topics
- Cheating in School
- Peer Pressure

30 Power Phrases about Substance Abuse

(Alcohol, Cigarettes and Drugs)

"Avoid using cigarettes, alcohol, and drugs as alternatives to being an interesting person." —Marilyn vos Savant

1. Be careful tonight. If your friends offer you a <drink/cigarette/drug>, just say you promised me you wouldn't.
2. Did you know that the teen brain is more sensitive than the adult brain to negative effects from alcohol? It can have a long-lasting negative impact on your memory and learning ability.
3. Do any of your friends drink, smoke, or do drugs?
4. Do kids have a hard time refusing <drinks/cigarettes/drugs> because they don't want to look uncool?
5. Do you know how alcohol/drugs affects our decision-making and self-control? It impairs judgment and leads you to do risky things like driving when you shouldn't, getting into a car with a drunk driver, or having unprotected sex—things you wouldn't even consider when sober.
6. Do you think it's OK to accept drinks from people you don't know or just met?
7. Going against the crowd can be scary, but it can be done. Remember, only a little over half of teens are current drinkers. That means that almost half aren't. It's up to you to decide where you stand.
8. Have fun tonight! Remember, I'm always happy to give you a ride—call or text me if your ride home has been drinking.
9. Have you heard about roofies and GHB? They're known as date rape drugs and can be put into drinks when they're unattended. They have no color, smell or taste. How can you protect yourself from date rape drugs? [ANSWERS: Open your own drink, keep it with you at all times, throw it out if you lose sight of it for even a second.]

10. I bet you're excited about starting high school, I'm excited for you. But I also know there's going to be some pressure to start drinking, smoking pot, or taking other drugs. Got any ideas what you'll do or say if that happens to you?
11. I know we talked about drinking and drugs when you were younger, but now that you're in <middle/high> school, you're more likely to find yourself in a place where kids are experimenting with some risky stuff. I want you to remember that I'm here for you and the best thing that you can do is just talk to me about what you hear or see. Don't think there's anything I can't handle or that you can't talk about with me, OK?
12. I trust you to make good decisions tonight. Let me know if you need anything. I'm here for you.
13. I'm really upset that you've been <smoking/drinking>. I want to give you the benefit of the doubt and assume that you were experimenting. The best thing that you can do now is really be straight with me, so for starters, tell me about what happened tonight. Then we need to review our rules about this.
14. If you aren't that concerned about putting your own life in danger, think about what it would be like if you were responsible for the death of a friend or some innocent person who was just trying to share the road. Could you really live with that?
15. If you ever get into a situation where kids are drinking and you feel uncomfortable, text me our code. No matter what the time and where you are, I will come and get you—no questions asked.
16. Remember our discussion about drinking. I love you too much to see anything bad happen to you.
17. The idea of drinking may seem like a fun way to let loose, but the fact is that alcohol is a depressant. Not only will you have a hangover in the morning, you'll be even more down.
18. What are your thoughts about binge drinking? I want to make sure that you understand that putting a large amount of alcohol into your body in a short period of time can lead to alcohol poisoning, which can lead to death. That is a medical fact.

19. What can you say if someone offers you a drink and you don't want it? How do you think they'll respond?
20. What do you consider to be social drinking?
21. What do you do when you are at a party and all your friends are drinking/smoking?
22. What do you know about the effects of alcohol?
23. What do you think about underage drinking?
24. What would you do if you were offered drugs?
25. When a person uses drugs and alcohol—especially a teen who's still growing—it changes how his brain works and can make him do really foolish things. Most people who use drugs and alcohol need a lot of help to get better.
26. When, if ever, you do drink? What is your purpose? To get drunk or buzzed? To relax? To be social or fit in? Is that a good reason?
27. Why do you think teens <drink/smoke/take drugs>?
28. You may think that you can handle alcohol, but drunk driving causes the deaths of 4,000 teens a year. You may think that you are the exception. But, trust me, all those kids thought that they were exceptions, too.
29. You probably know that parents talk to each other and find things out about what's going on at school. I heard that there are kids <selling/using> <type of drug>. Have you heard about this?
30. You'll have a lot of decisions to make about what you want to do in high school and you might even make some mistakes. Just know that you can talk to me about anything—even if you *do* make a mistake. I won't freak out. I want you to count on me to help you make smart decisions and stay safe, OK?

Did You Know?

Almost 40 percent of alcoholics begin drinking excessively between the ages of 15 and 19.[36] Research shows that parents are the number one reason that young people decide not to drink.[37]

Talking Tip

If you catch your teen with drugs, or even suspect her of using them, address it immediately. Some people quit using drugs after their teen years, but research shows that the younger people are when they try drugs, the more likely they are to end up as addicts.

Related Tools

- Drugs Cheat Sheet
- Reliable Resources Cheat Sheet
- Suicide Warning Signs Cheat Sheet
- Behavior Agreement

Related Chapters

- Buy More Time to Respond
- Clarify the Facts
- Confront a Teen Who's Lying
- Cool Down a Heated Situation
- Encourage Accountability
- Grab Your Teen's Attention
- Tackle Tough Topics
- Peer Pressure

24 Power Phrases about Suicide and Suicidal Thoughts

"Suicide is a permanent solution to a temporary problem." —Phil Donahue

1. Did something happen that made you start feeling this way?
2. Having thoughts of hurting yourself does not make you a bad person. Depression can make you think and feel things that are out of character.
3. I can't imagine how much you are hurting or how scared you must be to think that suicide is the only way out. I know you don't believe that things are going to get better, but they will. I'll help you find a way.
4. I know when you feel so much pain and hopelessness; suicide may feel like the only solution. But it isn't. I'm going to do everything I can to help you through this.
5. I love you too much to let you hurt yourself. I just want to let you know that I made an appointment for us to talk to a professional on <date/time>.
6. I may not be able to understand exactly how you feel, but I care about you and want to help.
7. I think that you feel there's no way out, but I know there are options that could help. I'd like you to at least try them.
8. I understand how bad things are for you right now. You are not alone. I am here to help you any way I can.
9. I want to help you come up with another way out of this.
10. I've noticed that you've been <warning sign>. Have you been having thoughts about trying to kill yourself?
11. I'm asking this because I love you and I'm worried about you: Have you had any thoughts of hurting yourself?
12. I've been concerned about you lately because <warning sign>. What's going on?
13. If you ever feel like you want to hurt yourself or like you don't want to live, please tell me, or call the doctor immediately. Sometimes

feelings can be overwhelming, and you feel like it might never get better. Suicide is permanent and feelings are not. We can help you to work through your feelings. Are you currently having any feelings of wanting to hurt yourself?

14. If you're afraid that you can't control yourself, make sure you are never alone. Stay in public places, hang out with friends or family members, or go to a movie—anything to keep from being by yourself and in danger.
15. If your feelings are uncontrollable, tell yourself to wait 24 hours before you take any action. During this time, try to talk to me or someone else you trust—as long as they are not another suicidal or depressed person.
16. If your feelings become so overwhelming that you can't see any solution besides harming yourself or others, you need to get help *right away*. If you don't feel comfortable talking to me or a friend, immediately call 1-800-273-TALK.
17. It sounds like you've given up. I had no idea things were so bad for you. When did you begin feeling like this?
18. No matter what, talk to someone, especially if you are having any thoughts of harming yourself or others. Asking for help is the bravest thing you can do, and the first step on your way to feeling better.
19. There is always another solution, even if you can't see it right now. Many kids who have attempted suicide (and survived) say that they did it because they mistakenly felt there was no other solution to a problem they were experiencing. At the time, they could not see another way out, but in truth, they didn't really want to die. Remember that no matter how horrible you feel, these emotions will pass.
20. When you say that you want to kill yourself or commit suicide, I take that very seriously. Have you thought about how you'd do it? Do you have the means? Have you decided when you'll do it? (If yes, take your teen to the nearest psychiatric facility or hospital emergency room immediately.)

21. When you want to give up, tell yourself that you will hold off for just one more day, hour, minute—whatever you can manage. Then immediately call me or someone else you trust.
22. You are not alone in this. I'm here for you. I do not want you to hurt yourself and I will do everything possible to keep you from committing suicide.
23. You may not believe it now, but the way you're feeling will change. It might help to talk about it.
24. You've been so unhappy lately. I know sometimes it may seem like things are so bad that there's no way out and life isn't worth living anymore. Have you been feeling like that? Please know, there is always another way. Let's talk about some solutions.

Did You Know?

You should always take suicidal talk or behavior seriously. It's not just a warning sign that the person is thinking about suicide—it's a cry for help. Call the suicide hotline ASAP: 1-800-273-8255.

Talking Tip

The words aren't as important as your show of concern. You can do this by:

- Being sympathetic, non-judgmental and calm
- Giving a hug
- Listening
- Offering hope

Related Tools

- Suicide Warning Signs Cheat Sheet
- Reliable Resources Cheat Sheet

Related Chapters

- Coax Your Teen to Open Up to You
- Comfort Your Teen
- Say "I Love You"
- Tackle Tough Topics
- Cutting and Self-Harm
- Depression
- Stress/Pressure to Succeed

22 Power Phrases about Technology Use and Safety

(Internet, Social Media and Texting)

"If you happen to tell me where you were born, your date of birth and that kind of information, then I'm 98 percent of the way to stealing your identity." —Frank Abagnale, infamous imposter

1. Can you show me how to update the privacy settings on my <social media> profile? What do you recommend I do to keep my personal information and location out of the hands of creepy strangers?
2. Do you feel like you can tell me if you ever have a problem online?
3. Has anyone at school posted something personal on social media that went viral? What happened? What would you do if that happened to you?
4. Has anyone ever asked you for your information or wanted you to get naked in front of them?
5. Have you seen this story about ...? What did you think about it? What would you do if you this happened to you?
6. Help me understand why <social media> is so important to you.
7. How are you protecting yourself against online sexual predators who target people on sites like this? How do you know if someone is a predator or not? You realize that they disguise their age, sex, and identity, right?
8. How do you determine who to friend and what information to share on <social media>?
9. I get why you want to be on <social media>, and I hope that you understand why I need to make sure you are using it responsibly. I know that it may seem like an intrusion on your privacy, but I want you to know that I'm going to periodically check out what you're doing on it until we're both confident that you're safe.
10. I want to be your friend on <social media>. Would that be OK with you?

11. If a stranger keeps trying to contact you or meet you in person, or sends you anything that makes you uneasy, tell me immediately and we'll report it on Cybertipline (www.cybertipline.com or 1-800-843-5678).
12. If there is anyone that you talk to online, or text, whom you feel you need to hide from me, I want you to seriously think about why. Your impulse to keep it from me is probably your gut telling you it's unsafe or unhealthy.
13. See anything interesting on <Instagram/Twitter/Pinterest/etc.> today?
14. Social media can get you into a lot of trouble if you don't use it responsibly. I want to trust you with it, but I also need to know you're safe. Let's establish some guidelines together and discuss how we can ensure that you're making wise choices.
15. Sometimes messages or images that you intend to be private can get into the wrong hands and be used to embarrass, intimidate, or humiliate you. Don't put anything out there that you wouldn't be comfortable having your entire class (and me) see.
16. What did you post on <social media> today?
17. What do you know about sexting? Do any of your friends do this? What do you think about that?
18. What sites do you like to visit?
19. What social media do the kids at school use these days? What do you think about it? Can you show me how it works?
20. What would you do if a stranger says he needs help and wants to use your phone?
21. What would you do if someone whom you met online asked to meet you in person? Do you know anyone who's done that?
22. Who are your friends on <social media>? How do you know them? Are you friends with anyone that you don't know in "real life"?

Did You Know?

Thirty-seven percent of all American teens have smartphones and about 3 in 4 teens (74 percent) ages 12 to 17 are "mobile Internet users" who say that they access the Internet on cell phones, tablets, and other mobile devices at least occasionally.[38]

Talking Tip

To teach teens to be safe online, make sure they know NOT to:

- Meet in person the strangers whom they chat with online
- Post their full name, address, phone number, or other personal information on their blog or social media site
- Share other information that can identify them (e.g., school, hangouts)
- Tell anyone their Internet, phone or email passwords (including best friends and boy/girlfriend—except you, the parent)

Related Tools

- Texting Red Flags
- Behavior Agreement
- Cell Phone Agreement
- Internet Use Agreement

Related Chapters

- Challenge a Sense of Entitlement
- Enforce Rules and Consequences
- Tackle Tough Topics
- Being Bullied
- Bullying Others
- Excessive Behavior
- Pornography

16 Power Phrases about Tolerance

(Prejudice, Stereotypes, Discrimination)

"No child is born a bigot. Hate is learned and there is no doubt it can be unlearned." —Carl Stern, Anti-Defamation League.

1. America was founded on the principle of tolerance—the acceptance of all people regardless of their <religious beliefs, skin color, sexual orientation, etc.> In fact, bringing together people with such diverse backgrounds enriches our culture and provides us with new ideas and perspectives. How can we respect these differences rather than ridicule them?
2. Do you think it's fair to judge a person or group based on something that they have no control over, such as skin color, ethnicity, or sexuality?
3. Have you ever felt excluded? How did it make you feel? Why do you think you were excluded? Was that a fair reason? Is it fair to be excluding <person> because of ...
4. "History doesn't always move as fast as we'd like. There are vestiges of slavery and Jim Crow. And although things have gotten enormously better, those biases are still there." –President Barack Obama
5. I know you were trying to be funny, but your remark/joke about ... upset me. It came across as hurtful toward <minority group>. Is that what you intended?
6. I noticed that you were looking at that person in the wheelchair. What do you think it's like to have to use a wheelchair to get around? What things do you think s/he has to do differently than us? What can s/he do the same way? Do you think being in a wheelchair makes her/him different than us? If so, how? How would you want people to treat you if you were in a wheelchair? Would you want their pity? Their help? Their admiration?
7. I'm wondering what led you to believe that about <person/group>.

8. In what ways do you think being <race, culture, religion, disability, etc.> makes <person> different from you? In what ways is s/he the same?
9. Some people believe that being homosexual is wrong, or that if someone really wanted to, they could become heterosexual. This is simply not true. Can you imagine if someone who was straight was expected to change whom they were attracted to and become gay? It doesn't seem too likely does it?
10. To be successful in life it's important to work well with all types of people. This means learning how to accept and appreciate people for who they are even if they are different from you.
11. We often don't think about how bad words can make someone feel. For example, people say, "that's so gay," or "that's retarded" to describe something negative. If someone who was gay or had a cognitive disability and constantly heard that, it could make him feel pretty bad about himself. What are some other words that you can use instead which aren't as hurtful?
12. What are some nonconfrontational ways to respond when you are called a hurtful name? What about when you hear a friend name-calling? What are the benefits and challenges of saying something to your friends in such a situation?
13. What does his/her <race/gender/sexual orientation, etc.> matter? Did I miss something?
14. Where is <person>'s family from? What do you know about that country? I'd like to learn more about it, what about you? Let's look it up online.
15. Why do you think s/he sounds different from you? Could it be that English isn't <person>'s first language? Imagine if you tried to speak <foreign language>, in her/his country. Do you think you'd sound "funny" to the people there? How would it make you feel if they laughed at you when you were doing your best to communicate?
16. You seemed uncomfortable around <person/group>. Why? It's common to feel uneasy around people that are different than us. The best thing to do is learn more about them. Do you have any questions that you want to ask me or look up?

Did You Know?

In 2002, the FBI reported that there were 7,462 hate crimes (crimes motivated by bias, prejudice, or bigotry) committed nationwide. Half of these crimes were committed by youths ages 15-24 [39]. These crimes were motivated by:

- 49% Race
- 19% Religion
- 17% Sexual Orientation
- 14% Ethnicity
- 1% Disability

Talking Tip

According to Partners Against Hate, it is essential that parents talk openly and honestly with their children about diversity-related topics. Minimizing differences or avoiding the topic altogether often sends the message that there's something "wrong" with people who are not like them. On the other hand, acknowledging differences and providing clear, accurate, and age-appropriate information about race, disabilities, sexual orientation, etc., helps teens become less judgmental and more accepting.

Related Tools

- Reliable Resources Cheat Sheet

Related Chapters

- Being Bullied
- Bullying Others
- Homosexuality
- Learning Disabilities
- Obesity & Weight
- Religion
- School Violence

10 Power Phrases about Toxic Relationships and Abuse

"It's not what you go through that defines you; you can't help that. It's what you do after you've gone through it that really tests who you are." —Kwame Floyd

1. Any time someone you're dating demeans you, forces you to do something you don't want to do, or hits you—get out of that relationship right away. Then talk to me or another adult you trust.
2. Have you witnessed dating violence at school or among friends? How does it make you feel? Were you scared?
3. How do you want to feel about yourself when you are with <name>?
4. I'm so sorry this happened to you. Thank you for telling me. I'm sure it wasn't easy. Sexual assault is a very serious issue, and I will help you get the help you need. Just know that you are not to blame for what happened. [National Sexual Assault Helpline: 1-800-656-HOPE (4673)].
5. This is not your fault. Nothing you did implied that you were "asking for it" or that you deserved it. Abuse is never deserved.
6. What do you think about how <name> treated <name> in that TV show/movie? Do you think her/his <actions/words> were justified? Would you go out with someone who treated you that way?
7. What would you do if you think your friend's <boy/girlfriend> isn't treating her/him right?
8. What would you do if your <boy/girlfriend> calls you to come over whenever you try to hang out with your friends?
9. What would you do if your friend yells at her/his <boy/girlfriend> in front of everyone at a party?
10. Would it be weird if someone you were dating texted you all day to ask you what you're doing?

Did You Know?

Abuse is more common in teen relationships than you might think. One in every 4 teens has been verbally, physically, emotionally, or sexually abused by the person they're dating and about 9 percent of teens are victims of physical violence from a dating partner each year.[40]

Talking Tip

Make sure that your teen is aware of these 12 red flags.

You may be in an abusive relationship if your boy/girlfriend:

1. Accuses or blames you for things you haven't done
2. Bosses you around
3. Checks your cell phone or email without permission
4. Is extremely jealous or insecure about your relationship
5. Keeps you from spending time with your family and friends
6. Frequently loses his temper with you
7. Makes you feel unsafe
8. Pressures or forces you to have sex with him
9. Pressures you to do things that you don't want to do (e.g., alcohol/drugs/break curfew)
10. Pushes, grabs, or touches you in a way that hurts or makes you feel uncomfortable
11. Puts you down and makes you feel bad about yourself
12. Says bad things about you and embarrasses you in front of other people

Related Tools

- Dating Agreement

Related Chapters

- Boost Your Teen's Self-Esteem
- Clarify the Facts
- Coax Your Teen to Open Up to You
- Comfort Your Teen
- Encourage Accountability
- Grab Your Teen's Attention
- Tackle Tough Topics
- Breaking Up and Broken Hearts
- Being Bullied
- Bullying Others
- Dating
- Extreme Emotions

20 Power Phrases about Underachievement

"It is our choices … that show what we truly are, far more than our abilities." —J.K. Rowling

1. Do you feel like there is too much pressure on you to achieve?
2. Given the gifts that you have, have you applied them as best you can?
3. Have you been feeling stressed-out about school lately?
4. How do you feel about these grades? What do you attribute them to?
5. I am surprised that you would get a low mark on this assignment. What can you learn from this assignment that will help you next time?
6. I have no doubt that you can successfully accomplish anything that you set your mind to as long as you're willing to work hard for it.
7. I notice that your performance hasn't been as good as usual and I'm wondering what's going on.
8. I noticed that your grades weren't as high as usual this semester—can we talk about it?
9. I realize that grades don't always reflect effort. Do you feel like you did the best you could <on that test/in that class>?
10. I value good grades because … and I want that for you. How important do you think grades are?
11. I'm wondering what you hoped to accomplish in that <class/game/on that test>. Are you happy with your performance? Is there anything that you could do differently next time?
12. I'm curious why you don't do as well in <subject> as you do in your other subjects. What do you think is the reason?
13. I'm not going to give up on you and I'm not going to let you give up on yourself. We don't want all that potential bottled up inside of you to go to waste. Let's find a way to let it out.
14. It seems like <subject> has been tripping you up lately, but your performance in all your other classes is still strong. I'd hate for that one class to undermine all your hard work. What can I do to help?

15. You usually do pretty well in <subject>. Is there some reason that your grades seem to be declining? Do you need some help?
16. I'm guessing that if you had put more effort into it, you could have done better. I'm disappointed that you decided not to try your best, but it's your grade and your choice to study hard or not.
17. What do you want to do after you graduate? What kind of grades and activities do you need to achieve that? Do you feel like you are on track to get what you want?
18. What will you do differently to stay on top of your grades? Let's pick one thing that you can do right now that will help you move in that direction.
19. What's getting in the way of you doing your work? How can you change that? Is there anything I can do to help?
20. Would a tutor help?

Did You Know?

Children who have dinner with their families and talk about school and grades actually do better in school overall.[41]

Talking Tip

Top 5 Things that Hold Teens Back

1. Boredom
2. Family issues
3. Low self-esteem
4. Peer pressure
5. Substance abuse

Related Tools

- Behavior Agreement
- Homework Agreement

Related Chapters

- Boost Your Teen's Self-Esteem
- Challenge a Sense of Entitlement
- Encourage Accountability
- Motivate Your Teen
- Grab Your Teen's Attention
- Tackle Tough Topics
- Cheating in School
- Excessive Behavior
- Peer Pressure

Cheat Sheets

Lying-Tells Cheat Sheet

If your teen does *several* of the following when talking to you, he may be lying:

Body tells

1. Makes little or no movement (aka pulling a possum)
2. Places a physical barrier (like a book, pillow, cup) between the two of you
3. Shrinks her posture to take up less physical space (legs and arms crossed)
4. Turns his body away from you

Eye tells

5. Blinks a lot more or a lot less than usual
6. Makes more eye contact than usual (almost stares you down)

Expression tells

7. Shows little full facial expression when talking
8. Timing is off between gestures and words (for example, says something sad, then frowns)
9. Unwittingly smirks, perhaps because he's amused about getting away with something

Feet tells

10. Crosses her ankles or nervously taps feet
11. Points his toes toward the door (a silent way of saying "Get me out of here!")

Hand tells

12. Fidgets with objects, wrings hands
13. Touches face, nose, mouth, ears
14. Turns palms upward (a subconscious way of asking you to believe her)

Language tells

15. Rattles off excessive, irrelevant details
16. Repeats your question verbatim (stalling technique)
17. Replaces contractions with formal language (for example "I did not ..." instead of "I didn't ...")
18. Uses hyperbole (such as, "I swear on my life," or "Never in a million years")
19. Uses phrases such as, "To tell the truth...," "To be perfectly honest...," and "Would I lie to you?"
20. Uses qualifying statements like, "As far as I remember ..."

Conversation Fuel

Not always sure how to start a productive conversation with your teen? Prepare yourself by writing down some fun, open-ended questions to ask the next time that you and your teen have some free time to talk. Then create some free time to talk! Here are a few questions to get you started:

1. Are you proudest of your accomplishments or your character? Which is more important?
2. Describe the coolest house/car/room/mythical creature you can imagine.
3. Do you believe in karma? Do you think you have good or bad karma?
4. If you could relive yesterday, what would you do differently?
5. If you could spend your Sunday afternoon doing whatever you want, what would you do?
6. Tell me five random facts that you find fascinating.
7. What are five small things you could do to make someone else's day better?
8. What are the three things you're most grateful for?
9. What are the most important qualities that you look for in a friend?
10. What can you do today that you weren't capable of doing a year ago?
11. What one article of clothing best describes you?
12. What song best describes your life right now?
13. What's been on your mind lately?
14. What's the best practical joke that you've ever done or had done to you?
15. What's the most interesting/funniest/craziest/lamest thing you heard today?
16. Which of Snow White's seven dwarves do you feel most like today?
17. Who inspires you the most? Why?
18. Would you rather be invisible or be able to read minds?
19. Would you rather be the smartest, most popular, or most attractive person you know?
20. If you could talk to one species of animals, what animal would you choose? What would you ask it?

Reliable Resources Cheat Sheet

Bullying and School Violence

- Action Work: http://www.actionwork.com/bullying.html
- American Psychology Association: http://www.apa.org/topics/bullying/index.aspx
- Stopbullying.gov: http://www.stopbullying.gov

Driver's Education

- American Automobile Association (AAA): http://teendriving.aaa.com/
- Centers for Disease Control (CDC): http://www.cdc.gov/motorvehiclesafety

Internet Safety

- FBI Parent Guide: http://www.fbi.gov/stats-services/publications/parent-guide/parent-guide
- National Crime Prevention Council (NCPC): http://www.ncpc.org/topics/internet-safety
- National Parent Teacher Association (PTA): http://www.pta.org

LGBT Support

- Gay, Lesbian and Straight Education Network (GLSEN): www.glsen.org
- High school gay-straight alliances
- Lyric: lyric.org
- Parents, Families and Friends of Lesbians and Gays (PFLAG): www.pflag.org
- Trevor Project: www.thetrevorproject.org

Mental and Emotional Support

- American Academy of Child & Adolescent Psychiatry (AACAP): http://www.aacap.org/
- American Foundation for Suicide Prevention (AFSP): http://www.afsp.org
- Helpguide.org: http://www.helpguide.org
- National Eating Disorder Association (NEDA): http://www.nationaleatingdisorders.org
- National Institute of Mental Health (NIMH): http://www.nimh.nih.gov/
- National Institute on Drug Abuse (NIH): http://www.drugabuse.gov
- National Sexual Assault Hotline: 1-800-656-HOPE (4673), www.RAINN.org
- Substance Abuse and Mental Health Services Administration (SAMHSA): http://www.samhsa.gov
- Suicide hotline: 1-800-273-8255
- TeensHealth: http://kidshealth.org/teen/

Money

10 fun, interactive websites help your teen learn about finances

- BizKids.com
- Italladdsup.org
- Kapitall.com
- Learn4Good.com Tycoon Games
- MoneyInstructor.com
- PracticalMoneySkills.com
- RichKidSmartKid.com
- SenseAndDollars.thinkport.org
- TheMint.org
- WhatsMyScore.org

Sex Education

- Centers for Disease Control and Prevention (CDC): www.cdc.gov
- Go Ask Alice: http://goaskalice.columbia.edu
- National Organization on Adolescent Pregnancy, Parenting, and Prevention (NOAPPP): www.noappp.org
- Office of Adolescent Health: www.hhs.gov
- Planned Parenthood: www.plannedparenthood.org
- Tanner Stage Calculator for Boys: http://growingupboys.info/Calculators/TannerStage.htm
- Tanner Stage Calculator for Girls: http://growingupgirls.info/Calculators/TannerStage.htm
- Teens WebMD: http://teens.webmd.com
- TeensHealth: http://kidshealth.org/teen/
- Teenwire.org: http://teenwire.org
- The Center for Young Women's Health: http://youngwomenshealth.org

Tolerance

- 101 Ways to Combat Prejudice: http://archive.adl.org/prejudice/closethebook.pdf
- Connecting With Kids: www.connectingwithkids.com
- Partners Against Hate: Partnersagainsthate.org
- Teaching Tolerance: www.tolerance.org
- Think Quest: www.thinkquest.org

Technology

- Internet Slang Dictionary & Translator: http://www.noslang.com
- Lingo 2 Word: http://www.lingo2word.com

Stages of Puberty Cheat Sheet

Tanner's 5 Stages of Puberty for Boys [42]

Stage	Development of...
1	Genitals: No pubertal development Pubic Hair: No pubertal development Growth: 2.0 to 2.4 inches per year
2	Genitals: Thinning and reddening of scrotum, testes growing Pubic Hair: Starts with a few lightly colored hairs Growth: 2.0 to 2.4 inches per year Other: Decrease in total body fat
3	Genitals: Penis growing (primarily in length), testes growing Pubic Hair: Spreads, darkens, and curls Growth: About 2.8 to 3.2 inches per year Other: Muscle mass increasing, voice breaks on occasion
4	Genitals: Penis growing, testes growing Pubic Hair: Adult-like (very little change between 4 and 5) Growth: 4.0 inches per year Other: Underarm hair, voice change, acne
5	Genitals: Adult genitalia Pubic Hair: Adult pubic hair Growth: Full height attained Other: Facial hair, muscle mass continues to increase beyond stage 5

Tanner's 5 Stages of Puberty for Girls

Stage	Development of...
1	Breasts: No development Pubic Hair: No development Growth: 2.0 to 2.4 inches per year Other: Ovaries growing
2	Breasts: Breast buds Pubic Hair: Starts with a few lightly colored hairs Growth: 2.8 to 3.2 inches per year Other: Clitoris and uterus growing
3	Breasts: Breast mounds (tissue grows beyond areola without contour separation) Pubic Hair: Spreads, darkens, and curls Growth: About 3.2 inches per year Other: Underarm hair begins growing and acne, vaginal discharge
4	Breasts: Breasts feature a projection of areola and papilla forms a secondary mound Pubic Hair: Adult-like (very little change between stages 4 and 5) Growth: 2.8 inches per year Other: First menstrual period
5	Breasts: Adult breast contour (projection of papilla only) Pubic Hair: Adult pubic hair Growth: Full height attained Other: Menstrual periods become regular

Birth Control Cheat Sheet

9 Most Common Birth Control Methods for Teens

Method	Description	How it's used	Effectiveness
Abstinence	Refraining from sexual activity.		100% effective Protects against STDs.
Birth control patch	Patch worn on the skin. Releases the same types of hormones as the birth control pill and is just as effective.	Changed only once a week for three weeks with a fourth week that is patch-free. Requires a prescription.	92% effective No STD protection
Birth control pill	Most common type of birth control pill uses the hormones estrogen and progestin to prevent ovulation.	Taken daily. Requires a prescription.	92% effective No STD protection
Diaphragm	A rubber dome	Placed over the cervix before sex. Often used with spermicide. Must be fitted by an M.D.	84% effective No STD protection
Emergency contraceptive (morning-after pill)	Pills that delay ovulation (the release of an egg during a girl's monthly cycle).	Depending on brand, can be taken up to 5 days after unprotected sex. Some require prescriptions if under the age of 16.	98% effective No STD protection

Female condom	A thin plastic pouch that lines the vagina.	Users grasp a flexible, plastic ring at the closed end to guide it into position. Can be put in place up to 8 hours before sex.	79% effective Some STD protection
Intrauterine device (IUD)	A T-shaped piece of plastic that makes it more difficult for sperm to fertilize the egg.	Placed inside the uterus by an M.D.	99% effective No STD protection
Male condom	The latex condom is the classic barrier method.	Placed over the penis before sex to prevent sperm from entering the woman's body, protecting against pregnancy and most STDs.	82% effective Some STD protection
Spermicides	A foam, jelly, cream, or film that contains a chemical that kills sperm.	Placed inside the vagina before sex. Often used with other forms of birth control methods. Some types must be put in place 30 minutes ahead of time.	70% effective No STD protection

Sexually Transmitted Diseases (STDs) Cheat Sheet

8 Most Common Teen STDs

STD	Description/Symptoms	How it's spread	Treatment
Chlamydia	Most common bacterial STD. No overt symptoms. If not treated can cause pelvic inflammatory disease (PID) or sterility.	Unprotected vaginal, oral, or anal sex	Antibiotics
Gonorrhea	A highly contagious bacterial infection affecting genitals, anus, or throat. Symptoms (if any) may include: vaginal/penile discharge, pelvic pain, and swollen testicles. Can cause sterility, arthritis, and heart trouble.	Unprotected vaginal, oral, or anal sex	Antibiotics
Hep-B (HBV)	A viral infection affecting the liver. No overt symptoms.	Unprotected vaginal, oral, or anal sex	Acute: rest, eating well, and lots of fluids. Chronic: anti-retroviral medications. Vaccinations.
Herpes	A viral infection of the genital areas. It can also infect the mouth and lips. Symptoms (if any) may include: cold sores, genital sores and blisters.	Unprotected vaginal, oral, or anal sex; skin-to-skin sexual contact; kissing	No cure, but medications can help treat symptoms and reduce outbreaks.

HIV	The human immunodeficiency virus (HIV) is a virus that weakens the immune system. Left untreated, it develops into AIDS, a fatal disease.	Unprotected vaginal, oral, or anal sex	No cure, however an Antiretroviral treatment can slow the progression of HIV and delay the onset of AIDS.
Human Papilloma Virus (HPV, genital warts)	A viral infection with over 40 types that can infect the genitals, anus, or throat. Symptoms (if any) may include: warts and cervical cancer.	Unprotected vaginal, oral, or anal sex; skin-to-skin sexual contact	No cure, but can treat symptoms. HPV vaccines are available for both males and females.
Syphilis	A highly contagious, progressive bacterial disease that can affect all parts of the body -- the brain, bones, spinal cord, heart, and reproductive organs. Symptoms (if any) may include: sores or rash.	Unprotected vaginal, oral, or anal sex	Antibiotics
Trichomoniasis (Trich)	A parasitic infection of the genitals. Symptoms (if any) may include vaginal/penile discharge and discomfort in the genital area.	Unprotected vaginal sex	Antibiotics

Drugs Cheat Sheet

7 Most Common Drugs Abused by Teens

Category	Description	Includes
Club drugs	Psychoactive drugs that come in the form of pills, liquid, or powder. Often used by teens at parties, clubs and "raves" (all night dance parties). Some are placed in alcoholic beverages and known as date rape drugs.	• Ecstasy. Also known as X, E, MDMA, hug drug, and love drug • GHB. Also known as Liquid X and date rape drug • Ketamine. Also known as K, special K, vitamin K, and super acid • Rohypnol. Also known as roofies and date rape drug
Hallucinogens	Compounds found in some plants that cause profound distortions in a person's perceptions of reality. Often taken orally.	• LSD. Also known as acid, blotter, dots, and trips • Mescaline • PCP. Also known as angel dust, whack, and embalming fluid • Psilocybin. Also known as mushrooms and 'shrooms
Inhalants: Also known as whippets (nitrous oxide) and poppers (amyl nitrites)	Everyday products that have mind-altering properties when inhaled through the nose or mouth (aka huffing). May also be taken by putting a chemical-soaked rag in the mouth or inhaling fumes from a balloon or a plastic or paper bag.	• Aerosol sprays (e.g., spray paint, hair spray, vegetable oil sprays) • Nitrates and gases (e.g., gasoline, lighter fluid, propane, refrigerants) • Paint thinners and removers • Wite-Out, glue, felt-tip markers, shoe polish

Prescription and over-the-counter (OTC) drugs	Because some medications have mind-altering properties, teens use them for reasons or in ways not prescribed. These are the most commonly abused substances by teens (14+) after marijuana and alcohol, probably because of their easy accessibility—your medicine cabinet.	• Depressants (e.g., Valium, Xanax). Also known as barbs, reds, yellow jackets; candy, downers, sleeping pills, tranks, and zombie pills • Opioids (e.g., OxyContin). Also known as hillbilly heroin, oxy, OC, oxycotton, percs, happy pills, and vikes • Stimulants (e.g., Ritalin). Also known as skippy, the smart drug, Vitamin R, bennies, black beauties, roses, hearts, speed, and uppers.
Marijuana: Also known as 420, Cannabis, weed, pot, bud, grass, herb, Mary Jane, MJ, reefer, skunk, boom, and ganja	From the hemp plant *Cannabis sativa*, which contains the mind-altering chemical delta-9-tetrahydrocannabinol (THC). Comes in the form of dried leaves, flowers, stems, and seeds and typically rolled in a thin paper and smoked, or inhaled through a pipe or bong.	• Hashish or hash. A concentrated form. • Hash oil. A sticky black liquid form.

Methamphetamine: Also known as speed, meth, glass, crystal and crank.	An extremely addictive stimulant drug that comes in the form of a white, odorless, bitter-tasting crystalline powder and is taken orally, smoked, snorted, or dissolved in water or alcohol and injected.	• Crystal meth. A pure, smokable form. Also known as ice.
Cocaine: Also known as coke, coca, C, snow, blow, Charlie and toot.	Addictive stimulant drug that often comes in a powdered form and is either inhaled through the nose (snorted) or dissolved in water and injected into the bloodstream.	• Crack. A rock crystal form that can be smoked. Also known as freebase cocaine, candy, and rock.

Social Media Cheat Sheet

10 Most Popular Social Networks/Apps Used by Teens in 2014 [43]

1. Facebook (https://www.facebook.com)
2. YouTube (https://www.youtube.com)
3. Instagram (http://instagram.com)
4. Snapchat (https://www.snapchat.com)
5. Pandora Radio (http://www.pandora.com)
6. Twitter (https://twitter.com)
7. Google+ (https://plus.google.com/)
8. Pinterest (http://www.pinterest.com)
9. Vine (https://vine.co)
10. Tumblr (https://www.tumblr.com)

Suicide Warning Signs Cheat Sheet

If your teen exhibits several of the behaviors listed below, she may be at risk for suicide. Seek professional help immediately or call the Lifeline at 1-800-273-TALK (8255). If you suspect your teen is suicidal and doesn't display any of the following symptoms, go with your instincts and get help.

- ❑ Appears depressed or sad most of the time. [Note: Untreated depression is the #1 cause of suicide.]
- ❑ Behaves impulsively and recklessly—as though he has a "death wish."
- ❑ Changes eating habits.
- ❑ Exhibits strong anger or rage.
- ❑ Experiences dramatic mood swings.
- ❑ Expresses excessive guilt or shame.
- ❑ Gives away prized possessions.
- ❑ Has a dramatic personality change.
- ❑ Loses interest in things she once cared about.
- ❑ Makes comments about feeling hopeless, helpless, or having no reason to live.
- ❑ Performs poorly at school.
- ❑ Researches ways to kill himself.
- ❑ Sleeps too little or too much.
- ❑ Talks about wanting to die or to kill herself.
- ❑ Talks or writes about death or suicide.
- ❑ Uses drugs or alcohol excessively.
- ❑ Withdraws from family and friends.
- ❑ Writes a will.

Texting Red Flags

In addition to the amount of time teens spend attached to their phones, parents worry about what they're texting about. Here are some texting and sexting abbreviations to watch out for.

If you see any of these red flags, try to stay calm. You don't want to ignore the situation, but getting angry, grounding your teen, and banning him from ever using his phone again will most likely create a power struggle and flip the focus from what's really important – the dangerous behavior – to a battle of wills. Not only will your ability to influence your teen positively be jeopardized, but also your teen will be motivated to find even sneakier ways to break the rules. (And believe me, he will!) Instead, use this as an opportunity to teach your teen how to make smart and safe choices on- and offline.

420 or **4life**	Marijuana
8	Oral sex
ASL(RP)	Age/Sex/Location/Race/Picture?
BYOB	Bring Your Own Bottle.
CD9 or Code9	Parents are around.
CU46	See you for sex.
D46	Do you want to have sex?
DUM	Do you Masturbate?
F/F or **F2F**	Face to Face
FWB	Friends With Benefits
GNOC	Get Naked On Camera
GNRN	Get Naked Right Now
GYPO	Get Your Pants Off
HSWM	Have Sex With Me
IWS	I Want Sex
JO	Jerk Off
KPC	Keeping Parents Clueless
LMIRL	Let's Meet In Real Life

MorF	Male or Female?
NIFOC	Naked In Front Of Camera
P911	Parent emergency
PAW/TAW	Parents Are Watching/Teachers Are watching
PIR	Parents In Room
POS/DOS/MOS/TOS	Parent/Dad/Mom/Teacher Over Shoulder
PRON	Porn
PRT	Party
RU18	Are you 18?
RUH	Are you Horny?
S2R	Send to Receive (pictures)
TDTM	Talk Dirty To Me
WTPA	Where's The Party At?
WYRN	What's Your Real Name?
YWS	You Want Sex

Parent/Teen Agreements

Why to use these agreements:

- ❑ Clearly define rules, consequences, rewards, and opportunities for restitution.
- ❑ Encourage collaboration.
- ❑ Facilitate teaching and discussion.
- ❑ Focus on specific behaviors and expectations.
- ❑ Help determine if the teen is ready for a new privilege.
- ❑ Hold you and your teen accountable.
- ❑ Increase student motivation and effort.
- ❑ Provide structure, routine, consistency, and organization.

When to use these agreements:

- ❑ When parents want to prevent power struggles.
- ❑ When parents want to provide clear guidelines.
- ❑ When teen earns a new privilege (e.g., driving, cell phone).
- ❑ When teen exhibits a persistent behavior problem.
- ❑ When teen and parents disagree on rules and consequences.

How to use these agreements:

1. Prepare the agreement.
   - ❑ Select an agreement and customize it to fit your needs. [Note: Keep the terms that work and modify to fit your personal situation and values, delete the terms that don't work, add terms if necessary, fill in the details.]
   - ❑ Put together a list of consequences, privileges, and rewards that your teen can select from. Make sure that they are motivating,

inexpensive, and are convenient for you. One of the biggest reasons that parents don't follow through with consequences is because they are too difficult to maintain.

2. Review the agreement with your teen.
   - ❑ Explain why the contract is necessary.
   - ❑ Lay down the rules for negotiation. Teens may negotiate the behavior, the rewards, and the criterion, but not the need for the contract itself.
3. Negotiate with your teen.
   - ❑ Explain each agreement term and its purpose. Describe the behavior that you want to work on with your teen and clarify if it's unclear to him.
   - ❑ Ask for you teen's input. Note: Teens often set unrealistically high expectations for themselves. Explain that it's important to start slowly; then gradually increase the expectations.
   - ❑ Collaborate to determine the specifics of each agreement term, such as expectations, time frames, consequences, privileges, and rewards.
4. Review and sign it together.
   - ❑ Make sure that you both understand and agree on all aspects of the contract.
   - ❑ Have all parties sign and date the agreement.
5. Post it.
   - ❑ Keep the agreement in an easily accessible or viewable location.
   - ❑ Refer to the agreement on a regular basis to remind all parties of its terms.
6. Follow through (the toughest part!)
   - ❑ To make the agreement effective, you must keep track of your teen's behavior, implement the agreed upon consequences when the contract is broken, and give the privileges and rewards when your teen abides by the terms.
7. Review the agreement terms on a regular basis.
   - ❑ Clarify guidelines if necessary.

- ❑ Increase specific privileges (e.g., curfew time) if the teen follows it for a given amount of time.
- ❑ Decrease privileges if the teen continuously breaks the agreed terms.
- ❑ Redefine consequences if they're too difficult for parents to enact or not effective for motivating the teen.

Examples of teen-appropriate consequences

The most effective consequences relate directly to the behavior you want to change, match the seriousness of the offense, and have a set end date. Natural consequences typically have the most impact, so use them whenever possible (i.e. when it doesn't put your teen or anyone else in harm's way). Remember, consequences should be used to teach, not shame or hurt. Consider the following:

- ❑ Appointment with a counselor or related professional
- ❑ Class or training related to the offense
- ❑ Extra chores
- ❑ A fine or price of incurred costs
- ❑ Loss or reduction of allowance
- ❑ Loss or reduction of privileges
- ❑ Writing a paper on a related topic
- ❑ Reduction in curfew
- ❑ Restricting where they can go/whom they can see
- ❑ Giving an apology (either written or verbally) to the person(s) negatively impacted by their actions

Examples of teen-appropriate privileges

Privileges are usually activities or things that your teen wants but doesn't need. They typically have a low monetary value. For example:

- ❑ Allowance/spending money

- ❑ Cell phone use
- ❑ Choice of family activity
- ❑ Computer time
- ❑ Extra chill time
- ❑ Gaming time
- ❑ iPad/iPod use
- ❑ Place/time to practice with their band
- ❑ Time with friends
- ❑ TV time

Examples of teen-appropriate rewards

Rewards are things or activities that your teen wants but doesn't need. They often have a higher monetary value than privileges. For example:

- ❑ App/game download
- ❑ Extended curfew
- ❑ Extra car time or gas money
- ❑ Extra sleep-in time
- ❑ Favorite meal or dessert
- ❑ Lunch or dinner out with a friend (or you)
- ❑ Mani/Pedi
- ❑ Movie tickets
- ❑ Music downloads
- ❑ New book
- ❑ New tool for their hobby
- ❑ Pizza and a movie night
- ❑ Redecorating their room
- ❑ Sleepover
- ❑ Staying up later
- ❑ Time with you

Allowance Agreement

This agreement defines and establishes allowance guidelines and associated expectations for our teen, ________________________________, as of ____________________, 20______.

Teen Expectations	
Amount	My allowance is: $__________ per week/month. I will be paid every ___________(day of week/month) on the condition that the below duties and behaviors are observed. When I receive my allowance, I will put the following % into each of the following categories: ____ % spend | ____ % save | ____ % invest | ____ % donate
Responsibilities	I understand that: ❑ It is my responsibility to keep track of where my money is at all times. ❑ I must budget my money to make sure that I can pay for all the items that I am responsible for. ❑ If I run out of money because I did not manage it well, then I cannot buy anything until my next allowance. ❑ If I'm having trouble managing my money or understanding my finances, I should ask my parent(s) or another trustworthy adult for help.
Duties	I understand that I must complete the following duties to earn my allowance: 1. 2. 3. 4. 5. (Note: This is not a finite list. My parent(s) have the authority to add additional tasks on occasion, but will give me a reasonable heads up if they do.)

Behaviors	I understand that I must exhibit the following behaviors to earn my allowance: 1. 2. 3. 4. 5.
Responsibilities	I agree that I am now responsible for purchasing the following items with my allowance (e.g., entertainment, games, makeup, gifts, etc.): 1. 2. 3. 4. 5.
Honor Code	I understand that I can NOT spend my allowance on the following items (e.g., candy, violent games, gambling, illegal substances, cigarettes, etc.): 1. 2. 3. 4. 5.
Penalties	I promise to follow the above rules and guidelines. I understand that if I break any of these terms, I am agreeing to accept one or more of the following penalties (without argument), based on the seriousness of my infraction: ☐ Lose all or some of my allowance for the week/month. ☐ Have to complete the following additional duties before receiving my base allowance:
Rewards	I understand that if I complete the following additional tasks, I can earn additional pay as follows: Task 1:______________________________ for $____________ Task 2:______________________________ for $____________ Task 3:______________________________ for $____________ I can also suggest additional tasks, although it is up to parental discretion if and how much I will be paid for them.

Parent Expectations	
Support	I promise to: ❑ Pay my teen $________ per week/month every ____________ of the week/month. ❑ Offer my teen an allowance that adequately covers the cost of the items that s/he is responsible for paying for. ❑ Teach my teen how to respect, understand, and manage money. ❑ Advise, but not dictate, how my teen spends her/his allowance. ❑ Not tack on additional tasks without first informing my teen. ❑ Pay my teen for additional tasks/responsibilities as stated in the Teen Expectations above, and take under serious consideration my teen's suggestions for other ways to earn money. ❑ Help my teen open up a bank account, save, invest, etc., or find another knowledgeable and trusted adult to help her/him.
Enforcement	I will: ❑ Be reasonable with consequences for violations of this agreement. ❑ Not get too upset when my teen makes a mistake. I realize that we all mess up, and the most important things are their safety and learning from these mistakes. ❑ Read and take under serious consideration any appeal or modification request to this agreement that my teen makes in a respectful and thoughtfully composed written document.

I, ______________________________________, understand that my allowance is a privilege that I must earn by being responsible and trustworthy. I acknowledge that the above rules and guidelines are established to teach me how to respect and manage money responsibly. In all cases of disagreement, my parent(s) have the authority to make the final decision. I have the right to appeal any decision or request modifications to this agreement in a respectful and thoughtfully composed written document, which will be reviewed by my parent(s), but will not guarantee a change.

______________________________ ____________________

Teen's Signature Date

I/we, the parent(s), agree to review the terms of this agreement on or before ________________<date>, with our teenager, ________________________________, and update it to reflect newly earned privileges and responsibilities, if necessary.

___________________________________ ____________________

Parent's Signature Date

___________________________________ ____________________

Parent's Signature Date

Behavior Agreement

This agreement defines and establishes behavior expectations and goals for our teen, ______________________________________, as of ____________________, 20______.

	Teen Expectations	Possible consequences	Possible rewards
Expectation Instructions	**Define behavior** that you want to improve (e.g., Alcohol/drug use, anger issues, breaking curfew, bullying, conflict resolution, dishonesty, disrespect, poor school performance, shoplifting, smoking). **Clarify goals** clearly and concisely. Set your teen up for success by making them attainable and measurable (e.g., bring science grade up from a D to a C on next report card, quit smoking by Oct. 31). **Provide specific tasks** that will help your teen achieve these goals. Break the goals into concrete, small steps that build on one another. For example, learn and practice 1 new anger management technique a month; set aside 1 hour a day for homework).	List 1-3 consequences that relate as closely to the behavior as possible. Natural consequences often work best (as long as there is no risk of harm.)	List 1-3 rewards to encourage consistency (e.g., Desired behavior for 7 days in a row= 1 extra hour playing video games.
Behavior 1	Behavior: Goal: Tasks:	1. 2. 3.	1. 2. 3.

<table>
<tr><td>Behavior 2</td><td>Behavior:
Goal:
Tasks:</td><td>1.
2.
3.</td><td>1.
2.
3.</td></tr>
<tr><td>Behavior 3</td><td>Behavior:
Goal:
Tasks:</td><td>1.
2.
3.</td><td>1.
2.
3.</td></tr>
<tr><td>Behavior 4</td><td>Behavior:
Goal:
Tasks:</td><td>1.
2.
3.</td><td>1.
2.
3.</td></tr>
<tr><td>Honor Code</td><td colspan="3">I promise to:
❑ Accept the consequences as described above if I fail to achieve these goals.
❑ Inform my parents immediately if I don't think I can reach a goal within the given time frame, so we can find an alternative solution.
❑ Not tell my parent(s) that I have completed a task when I have not.
❑ Try my best to accomplish the goals above.</td></tr>
<tr><td>Attitude</td><td colspan="3">I understand that:
❑ I may be rewarded for achieving the goals 1) as described above in "Behaviors 1-4" and 2) with increased confidence, self-esteem, and pride earned from my own accomplishments.
❑ I will be held accountable for the impact that my behavior has on others.
❑ Only I have control over my behavior and that it is unproductive to blame others for my mistakes.
❑ The above goals and tasks have been put in place because my parent(s) love me and want to help me develop the skills, knowledge, and personality traits that will allow me to be healthy, happy, and successful now and throughout my life.</td></tr>
</table>

Parent Responsibilities	
Support	I promise to: ❑ Be a good role model by demonstrating the same behaviors expected of my teen. ❑ Be available to answer any questions that my teen has about the Teen Expectations above. ❑ Do everything in my power to help my teen succeed by using love, patience, and emotional support. ❑ Extend more privileges/freedoms to my teen as s/he proves to be trustworthy, respectful, and responsible. ❑ Provide my teen with the tools and support s/he needs to achieve the above goals.
Enforcement	I will: ❑ Be reasonable with consequences for violations of this contract. ❑ Not get overly upset when my teen makes a mistake or backtracks. I realize that teens will mess up, and the most important things are their safety and learning from these mistakes. ❑ Reward my teen when s/he achieves her/his goals as described above. I realize that the success of this agreement depends on me following through with my responsibilities and promises as stated above. ❑ Read and take under serious consideration any appeal or modification request to the Teen Expectations that my teen makes in a respectful and thoughtfully composed written document.

I, ______________________________, promise to abide by the above rules and regulations and will willingly face the penalties we have agreed upon if I break any of them. In all cases of disagreement, my parent(s) have the authority to make the final decision. I have the right to appeal any decision or request modifications to this agreement in a respectful and thoughtfully composed written document, which will be reviewed by my parent(s), but will not guarantee a change.

______________________________ ____________________

Teen's Signature Date

I/We, the parents, agree to review the terms of this agreement on or before ________________<date>, with my teenager, ___________________________, and update it to reflect newly earned privileges and responsibilities, if necessary.

___________________________________ ____________________

Parent's Signature Date

___________________________________ ____________________

Parent's Signature Date

Cell Phone Agreement

This agreement defines and establishes cell phone use guidelines and associated expectations for our teen, ________________________________ __________, as of ______________________, 20______.

<table>
<tr><th colspan="2">Teen Expectations</th></tr>
<tr><td>Usage</td><td>I will:
❑ NOT use my phone:
o between ______ pm and _______ am on school nights or
o between ______ pm and _______ am on non-school nights
unless given permission by my parent(s) or in an emergency.
❑ Dock my cell phone at the family charging station located at __________________________ during <family dinner/homework time/family time/bedtime/________________>.
❑ Respond to all calls and texts from my parent(s) within ___ minutes of receiving them.
❑ Not buy/download anything online without parental permission.
❑ Not go over my share of our plan's coverage, which is _____ minutes/month and _______ texts/month.</td></tr>
<tr><td>Care</td><td>I am responsible for:
❑ Knowing where my phone is at all times.
❑ Keeping my phone in good condition.
❑ Making sure my phone is charged.</td></tr>
<tr><td>Safety</td><td>I promise to:
❑ Protect my privacy, which means NEVER sharing:
o My full name, address/location, age, school, phone number or other personal information to anyone I don't know.
o My password to anyone (including friends), except my parents.
❑ Alert my parents if I am being cyber-bullied or receive suspicious or alarming phone calls or text messages.
❑ NEVER meet someone face to face that I meet online.
❑ NEVER text while driving or ride in a car with someone who does.</td></tr>
</table>

<table>
<tr><td>Etiquette</td><td>I will:
❑ NOT use my phone during meals or family time.
❑ Obey all cell phone rules my school has while on school property (includes the bus).
❑ NOT use my cell phone disruptively in public places (such as churches, restaurants, schools, etc.)
❑ Turn off/get off my phone immediately if asked – and with a respectful attitude.
❑ When I am with others, make the people I am with my priority.</td></tr>
<tr><td>Honor Code</td><td>I will NOT:
❑ Send, forward or respond to inappropriate, hurtful or threatening text messages, emails, images, videos or posts.
❑ Use my cell phone to take pictures or video of nudity, sexually suggestive activity, violence or other unlawful activity.
❑ Take, send or post any photos of anyone without that person's permission.
❑ Withhold my passwords or access to my texts, call-log, and privacy settings from my parents.</td></tr>
<tr><td>Penalties</td><td>I promise to abide by the above rules and guidelines. I understand that if I break any of these terms, I am agreeing to accept one or more of the following penalties (without argument), based on the seriousness of my infraction as determined by my parent(s):
❑ Lose phone privilege for ________ days to _________ weeks.
❑ Reduce daily cell phone use to _____ minutes a day.
❑ Pay overage/purchasing costs incurred.
❑ Pay up to ______ in replacement/repair costs.
❑ Give a written or verbal apology
❑ Write a ______ word paper about cell phone safety.</td></tr>
<tr><td>Rewards</td><td>If I prove that I am a safe and responsible cell phone user by following the terms of this agreement for _______ consecutive days, I may earn one of the following rewards:</td></tr>
</table>

Parent Expectations	
Privacy	I promise to: ❑ Respect my child's privacy when s/he is talking or texting on the phone. ❑ NOT invade my child's privacy by reading text messages or looking through call logs without telling my child first. ❑ Let my teen know if I have concerns, and look through her/his phone with her/him.
Support	I will: ❑ Support my teen when s/he alerts me to an alarming voice or text message. ❑ Do everything I can to teach my teen to use her/his phone responsibly and safely. ❑ Sit down and talk to my teen about any mistakes s/he makes so we can both learn from it and move on. ❑ Pay $______/month for my teen's cell phone use. ❑ Alert my teen if our cell phone plan changes and impacts her/his usage.
Enforcement	I will: ❑ Give my teen ____ warning(s) before I enact a penalty. ❑ Match the penalty to the infraction (behavior and level of seriousness). ❑ Give my teen the benefit of the doubt and listen to her/his side of the story before determining the penalty. ❑ Read and take under serious consideration any appeal or modification request to this agreement my teen makes in a respectful and thoughtfully composed written document.

I, ____, understand that having a cell phone is a privilege that I must earn by being responsible and trustworthy. I acknowledge that the above rules and guidelines are established to keep me safe and teach me how to use my phone responsibly. In all cases of disagreement, my parent(s) have the authority to make the final decision. I have the right to appeal any decision or request modifications to this agreement in a respectful and thoughtfully composed written document, which will be reviewed by my parent(s), but will not guarantee a change.

______________________________ __________________

Teen's Signature Date

I/we, the parents, agree to review the terms of this agreement with my teenager on or before ____________<date>, and update it to reflect any new privileges my teen has earned by consistently abiding by the Teen Expectations above.

______________________________ __________________

Parent's Signature Date

______________________________ __________________

Parent's Signature Date

Curfew Agreement

This agreement defines and establishes curfews and associated expectations for our teen, ____, as of ______________________, 20______.

Teen Expectations

Guidelines

I understand that:

- ❑ My curfew is ________p.m. on school nights and ________p.m. on non-school nights.
- ❑ If I want to request an exception for a specific event, I must provide a valid reason at least ____ hours before going out. My parent(s) will take it under consideration and I will accept the answer—even if it's no.
- ❑ If I'm caught sneaking out, I am in violation of my curfew.

Responsibilities

I promise to:

- ❑ Let my parent(s) know who I'm with, where I'll be, and how I'm getting there when I go out.
- ❑ Call home if a circumstance beyond my control prevents me from getting home by my curfew. I understand that if I call early enough and explain the situation, it will NOT be considered a break in the contract.
- ❑ Check in with my parent(s) immediately if plans change.
- ❑ Provide a phone number where I can be reached and respond to a call or text from my parent(s) within ____ minutes.
- ❑ Use good judgment while out with my friends.

Contacts

If I can't reach my parent(s) when I need help, the following people have agreed to help me with advice or a ride home regardless of the time or circumstances. I have programmed this information into my phone.

Name:	Cell phone #:
Name:	Cell phone #:
Name:	Cell phone #:

Penalties	I promise to follow the above rules and guidelines. I understand that if I break any of these terms, I am agreeing to accept one or more of the following penalties (without argument), based on the seriousness of my infraction as determined by my parent(s): ❑ Move my curfew back to ________p.m. for ________ days. ❑ Restrict where I can go to the following location(s) for ______ days. ____ ❑ Restrict who I can hang out with after school and on weekends to the following people for _____ days. ____ ❑ Give a written/verbal apology to anyone I may have negatively affected. ❑ Research and write a ______ word paper about the importance of curfews.
Rewards	I understand that if I show I am trustworthy and responsible by meeting my curfew ____ times in a row, I may earn a later curfew and/or one or more of the following rewards:

Parent Expectations

Support	I promise to: ❑ Set realistic curfews, but also tell my teen that if s/he is running late, it's always better to drive safely than speed to make up the minutes. ❑ Agree that a call from my teen to provide her/him a ride will not count as a violation of this contract. ❑ Sit down and talk to my teen about any mistakes s/he makes so we can both learn from them and move on. ❑ Extend more privileges/freedoms to my teen as s/he proves to be trustworthy and responsible by abiding by curfew and the Teen Expectations stated above.

Enforcement	I will: ❑ Match the penalty to the infraction (behavior and level of seriousness). ❑ Give my teen the benefit of the doubt and listen to her/his side of the story before determining the penalty. ❑ Give my teen ____ warning(s) before I enact a penalty. ❑ Read and take under serious consideration any appeal or modification request to this agreement that my teen makes in a respectful and thoughtfully composed written document.
Safety Promise	I/we ______________________, promise to pick you up without question if you call because you're in a situation that threatens your safety. It doesn't matter where you are, what time it is or what the situation is. Because I want you to always feel comfortable calling me when you need help, I promise not to yell at you or be angry when you do. We will postpone discussions about that situation until we can both discuss the issues in a calm, caring way.

I, ______________________________________, understand that going out with my friends is a privilege that I must earn by being responsible and trustworthy. I acknowledge that the above rules and guidelines are established to keep me safe and teach me to be responsible. In all cases of disagreement, my parent(s) have the authority to make the final decision. I have the right to appeal any decision or request modifications to this agreement in a respectful and thoughtfully composed written document, which will be reviewed by my parent(s), but will not guarantee a change.

________________________________ ____________________

Teen's Signature Date

I/we, the parent(s), agree to review the terms of this agreement with my teenager on or before _________________<date>, and update it to reflect any new privileges my teen has earned by consistently abiding by the above terms.

______________________________ __________________

Parent's Signature Date

______________________________ __________________

Parent's Signature Date

Dating Agreement

This agreement defines and establishes dating guidelines and associated expectations for our teen, ______________________________________, as of ______________________, 20______.

Teen Expectations

Guidelines

I understand that I'm allowed to:

- ❑ Go on group dates once I'm _____ years old.
- ❑ Go on one-to-one dates once I'm ______ years old.
- ❑ Date people that are no more than ___ years older or ___years younger than I am.
- ❑ Go on ______ dates per week. (This includes visiting at each other's homes but not group or school outings.)
- ❑ Stay out until my curfew. At that time, I will be home with the door shut and my date gone.

Safety

I promise to:

- ❑ Immediately call my parent(s) no matter where I am or what I am doing if I find myself in a situation in which my safety is in danger or makes me uncomfortable (e.g. abuse, alcohol, drugs, unwanted pressure).
- ❑ Introduce all new dates to my parent(s) before I go out with her/him.
- ❑ Leave my cell phone on and answer it immediately if my parent(s) call, or respond within _____ minutes if they text.
- ❑ Make sure that I'm clear about where my boundaries are and am confident about saying "no" if necessary.
- ❑ NEVER give my personal information to anyone I "meet" online nor meet her/him face to face.
- ❑ NOT take anything (e.g., alcohol/drugs) that could impact my judgment and jeopardize my safety.
- ❑ NOT take or share pictures or video of nudity or sexually suggestive activity involving myself or anyone else via text, email, Snapchat, Instagram, Facebook, FaceTime, Skype or any other method.
- ❑ Obey all traffic rules if I am driving.

	❑ Tell my parent(s) the names of all the people that will be on my group date. ❑ Tell my parent(s) where I am going to be and with whom for the entire time I am gone. If plans change, I will inform my parent(s) immediately. ❑ Use good judgment and discuss with my parents immediately all serious or dangerous matters that may arise while dating.
Contacts	If I can't reach my parent(s) when I need help, the following people have agreed to help me with advice or a ride home regardless of the time or circumstances. I will program this information into my phone: Name: Cell phone #: Name: Cell phone #: Name: Cell phone #:
Restrictions	I will not: ❑ Let dating interfere with the following activities/responsibilities: ❑ Participate in the following activities while on a date: ❑ Visit the following places while on a date:
Honor Code	I promise to: ❑ Never attempt to pressure or force my date to do something s/he doesn't want to do. I understand that "no" always means "no." ❑ Talk to my parents or another trusted adult if I ever have any questions about dating. ❑ Treat my date with the utmost respect.
Understanding	I have discussed with my parent(s) and understand: ❑ The emotional impact of dating ❑ Sex and sexuality ❑ Birth control and pregnancy ❑ STDs

Penalties	I promise to follow the above rules and guidelines. I understand that if I break any of these terms, I am agreeing to accept one or more of the following penalties (without argument), based on the seriousness of my infraction as determined by my parent(s): ❑ Loss of dating privileges for _______ days. ❑ Move my curfew back to _______ p.m. for _______ days. ❑ Loss of cell phone privileges for _______ days. ❑ Require a chaperone on dates for _______ days. ❑ Restrict dates to following locations for _______ days: ____ ❑ Give a written/verbal apology to anyone I may have negatively effected. ❑ Research and write a ______ word paper about <dating/respect/ domestic violence).
Rewards	I understand that if I show that I am trustworthy and responsible by abiding by the above terms for ____ consecutive weeks, I may earn the following additional privileges and/or rewards:

Parent Expectations	
Privacy	I promise to respect my teen's privacy when s/he is: ❑ On a date—as long as my teen has introduced me to her/his date and keeps me informed of their plans. ❑ Talking and texting on the phone—unless s/he gives me a reason to suspect inappropriate or dangerous behavior.
Support	I will: ❑ Do my best to model and teach my teen how to treat people with respect and honor her/his own boundaries as well as her/his date's. ❑ Listen to my teen and help her/him through the emotional ups and downs of dating and relationships without judgment or criticism. ❑ Make myself available to answer any of my teen's questions about dating, relationships, sex, sexuality, birth control, STDs, or anything else s/he wishes to discuss. ❑ Respect that my child is becoming a young adult and wants the privilege of dating openly.

<table>
<tr><td>Enforcement</td><td>I will:
❑ Give my teen ___ warning(s) before I enact a penalty.
❑ Match the penalty to the infraction (behavior and level of seriousness).
❑ Give my teen the benefit of the doubt and listen to her/his side of the story before determining the penalty.
❑ Read and take under serious consideration any appeal or modification request to this agreement that my teen makes in a respectful and thoughtfully composed written document.</td></tr>
<tr><td>Safety Promise</td><td>I promise to pick you up without question if you call because you're in a situation that threatens your safety. It doesn't matter where you are, what time it is, or what the situation is.

Because I/we want you to always feel comfortable calling me when you need help, I promise not to yell at you or be angry when you do. We will postpone discussions about that situation until we can both discuss the issues in a calm, caring way.</td></tr>
</table>

I, ____, understand that dating is a privilege that I must earn by being responsible and trustworthy. I acknowledge that the above rules and guidelines are established to keep me safe and teach me to be responsible. In all cases of disagreement, my parent(s) have the authority to make the final decision. I have the right to appeal any decision or request modifications to this agreement in a respectful and thoughtfully composed written document, which will be reviewed by my parent(s), but will not guarantee a change.

____ ________________________

Teen's Signature Date

I/we, the parent(s), agree to review the terms of this agreement on or before ________________<date>, with our teenager, ____________________________, and update it to reflect newly earned privileges and responsibilities, if necessary.

Parent's Signature	Date
Parent's Signature	Date

Driving Agreement

This agreement defines and establishes driving guidelines and associated expectations for our teen, ______________________________, as of ____________________, 20______.

Teen Expectations	
Usage	I promise to: ❑ Only drive the following car(s):__________________________ ❑ Get permission from my parent(s) *every* time I drive. ❑ Tell my parent(s) where I'm going, how I'm getting there, who will be in the car with me and when I'll be home. ❑ Respect the curfew of_______ p.m. on school nights and _______ p.m. on non-school nights ❑ Call home if I expect to be more than _____ minutes late. ❑ Never let anyone else drive my car.
Care	I will: ❑ Take good care of the car and keep it free of clutter and trash. ❑ Make sure that there is at least ¼ tank of gas in the car when I'm done with it. ❑ Contribute $______/month toward gas, maintenance, and insurance.
Traffic Rules	I will: ❑ Always wear a seatbelt and make my passengers buckle up. ❑ Obey all speed limits, stop signs, traffic signals, and the rules of the road. ❑ Not drive aggressively (e.g., speeding, tailgating, cutting others off). ❑ Not drive with more than _____ passengers in the car. ❑ Not use alcohol or drugs before or when I'm driving. ❑ Not allow any alcohol or drugs in my car. ❑ Not ride in a car where any alcohol or drug use is occurring.

<table>
<tr><td>Safety</td><td>I will:
❑ Keep both hands on the wheel at all times (which means I won't use my cell phone, eat, drink, mess with the radio, etc., while driving.)
❑ Keep my eyes on the road at all times (which means I won't read texts, goof off, etc.).
❑ Pull over to a safe location if I need to text or talk on the phone.
❑ Not wear headphones or play the music so loud I can't hear noises like sirens and car horns.
❑ Not drive when angry, upset, or overly tired.
❑ Not put others or myself at risk by driving in extreme conditions (heavy rain, snow, etc.).
❑ Not race or engage in stunts or other risky behavior behind the wheel.
❑ Call my parent(s) for a ride home if I am impaired in any way that interferes with my ability to drive safely.
❑ Not pick up hitchhikers or allow anyone I don't know in the car.
❑ Keep my cell phone charged and with me at all times.</td></tr>
<tr><td>Contacts</td><td>If I can't reach my parent(s) when I need help, the following people have agreed to help me with advice or a ride home regardless of the time or circumstances. I will program this information into my phone:
Name: Cell phone #:
Name: Cell phone #:
Name: Cell phone #:</td></tr>
<tr><td>Honor Code</td><td>I will:
❑ Not conceal traffic violations, tickets, citations, warnings, etc., from my parent(s).
❑ Tell my parent(s) if the car has been damaged (scratched, dented, etc.) while in my care.
❑ Call my parent(s) immediately if I get into an accident, no matter how minor.</td></tr>
</table>

Penalties	I promise to follow the above rules and guidelines. I understand that if I break any of these terms, I am agreeing to accept one or more of the following penalties (without argument), based on the seriousness of my infraction as determined by my parent(s). ❑ Lose driving privileges for _____ days to ______ weeks. ❑ Move curfew back to ______p.m. for ______ days. ❑ Restrict driving destinations to the following locations for _______ days. ____ ❑ Ban the following driving destinations for ______ days. ____ ❑ Ban the following passengers for ______ days. ____ ❑ Attend the following class/intervention/therapy. _____________ _______________________ ❑ Pay an extra $______ toward car wash or gas. ❑ Pay for citations/tickets/damages incurred. ❑ Research and write a ______word paper about driving safety.
Rewards	I understand that if I show I am trustworthy and responsible by following the above terms for ______ days/weeks in a row, I may earn additional driving privileges and/or one or more of the following rewards:

Parent Expectations	
Support	I promise to: ❑ Help my teen learn how to drive using love, patience and support. ❑ Let my teen drive to local places with me as the passenger so I can see first-hand how s/he is driving. ❑ Be available to answer any specific driving questions. ❑ Extend more privileges to my teen as s/he proves to be a safe and responsible driver.

Safety	I will: ❑ Be a good role model by obeying all traffic laws, always wearing my seat belt, never drinking and driving, and not using illegal or distracting electronic devices. ❑ Teach my teen what to do in an emergency (change a tire, jump-start car, exchange insurance information, respect police officers, etc.). ❑ Keep the car stocked with emergency items including: Jumper cables, flashlight, batteries, road flares, first aid kit, spare tire and jack, gloves, a screwdriver, and a road safety guide.
Enforcement	I will: ❑ Set realistic curfews, but also tell my teen that if s/he is running late, it's always better to drive safely than speed to make up time. ❑ Be reasonable with consequences for violations of this contract. ❑ Not get too upset when my teen makes a mistake or has an accident. I realize that teen drivers will mess up, and the most important things are their safety and learning from these mistakes. ❑ Not count it as a violation if my teen calls to request a ride for safety reasons. ❑ Read and take under serious consideration any appeal or modification request to this agreement that my teen makes in a respectful and thoughtfully composed written document.
Safety Promise	I promise to pick you up without question if you call because you're in a situation that threatens your safety. It doesn't matter where you are, what time it is or what the situation is. Because I want you to always feel comfortable calling me when you need help, I promise not to yell at you or be angry when you do. We will postpone discussions about that situation until we can both discuss the issues in a calm, caring way.

I, ________________________________, understand that driving is a privilege that I must earn by being responsible and trustworthy. I acknowledge that the above rules and guidelines are established to keep me safe and teach me how to drive responsibly. In all cases of disagreement, my parent(s) have the authority to make the final decision. I have the right to appeal any decision or request modifications to this agreement in a respectful and thoughtfully composed written document, which will be reviewed by my parent(s), but will not guarantee a change.

________________________________ ____________________

Teen's Signature Date

I/we, the parent(s), agree to review the terms of this agreement on or before ________________<date>, with our teenager, ______________________________, and update it to reflect newly earned privileges and responsibilities, as appropriate.

________________________________ ____________________

Parent's Signature Date

________________________________ ____________________

Parent's Signature Date

Homework Agreement

This agreement defines and establishes homework and school performance expectations for our teen, ____,
as of ________________________, 20_______.

Teen Expectations

Grade Goals

My grade goals for this upcoming semester are:
(Note: expectations should be attainable—either maintain or bring it up by one grade at a time.)

Art _____	Music ______
English _____	Physical Education _____
Health _____	Science _____
Foreign Language _____	Social Studies _____
Math _____	Other ______________________________

Homework time

I promise to:

- ❑ Dedicate a minimum of _____ minutes a day to homework.
- ❑ Use homework time for studying, reviewing or reading if there are no outstanding assignments.
- ❑ Do my homework in one of the following locations: kitchen, family room, dining room, study, deck/porch. (Note: Avoid studying in the bedroom—too many distractions.)
- ❑ Dock my cell phone in the family charging station during homework time.
- ❑ NOT play TV, loud music, games, etc., during homework time.
- ❑ Complete my homework before I watch TV, text or call my friends, play on the computer/video games, or go out.

Assignments

I will:

- ❑ Keep and fill out an assignment logbook daily.
- ❑ Make sure I know when my assignments are due.
- ❑ Take responsibility for handing in assignments on time.

Help	I will: ❑ Let my parent(s) and/or teacher(s) know if I do not understand an assignment, or am having trouble keeping up in class. ❑ Ask (and allow) my parent(s) to help me understand material that I am struggling with. ❑ Let my parent(s) know at least ____ day(s) in advance if I need additional school supplies to complete an assignment.
Honor Code	I promise to: ❑ Do my homework to the best of my ability. ❑ Not tell my parent(s) I have completed an assignment when I have not. ❑ Show my grades and report cards to my parent(s). ❑ Never, ever cheat. I understand that cheating on my homework and tests is unacceptable. (This includes copying other people's work, having someone else complete my assignments for me, using a cheat sheet, helping other people cheat, etc.)
Attitude	I understand that: ❑ The above terms have been put in place because my parent(s) love me and want me to get the most that I can out of school, learn to work hard, and take pride in my accomplishments. ❑ The effort that I make (e.g., studying) is more important than the end result (grade). ❑ My parent(s) are trying to help me, and taking my frustration and anger out on them is unproductive and will only make things more difficult for me. ❑ I will be held accountable for my actions and natural consequences that occur if I do not do my homework, study, or keep up my grades.

Penalties	I promise to follow the above rules and guidelines. I understand that if I break any of these terms, I am agreeing to accept one or more of the following penalties (without argument), based on the seriousness of my infraction as determined by my parent(s): ❑ Reduce cell phone privileges to ______ hours a day for ______ days. ❑ Reduce TV/video game/computer privileges for ______ days or until I complete the following assignments/projects: ❑ Move my curfew back to ______p.m. for ______ days. ❑ Meet with a tutor for ______ times a week for ______ weeks. ❑ Write a ______ word paper about importance of education/study habits/etc.
Rewards	I understand that if I show that I am trustworthy and responsible by following the above terms for ______ days in a row, I may earn additional privileges and/or one or more of the following rewards:

Parent Responsibilities	
Support	I promise to: ❑ Be available to assist my teen during homework time. ❑ Seek outside help (e.g., tutor) if requested by my teen. ❑ Provide my teen with a quiet place to study that's free from distractions. ❑ Provide transportation to the library or other places to assist in homework completion. ❑ Make sure that my teen has the supplies that s/he needs to finish assignments (as long as s/he gives me notice of a day or more before they are needed). ❑ Coach my teen by quizzing, prompting, showing her/him where and how to do research, etc., but only if it's requested by my teen. ❑ NOT to DO the assignments for my teen. ❑ NOT over-schedule my teen with so many extracurricular activities that s/he cannot keep up with her/his homework assignments. ❑ Offer my child positive encouragement and acknowledge her/his efforts.

Enforcement	I will: ❑ Be reasonable with consequences for violations of this contract. ❑ NOT get too upset when my teen makes a mistake. I realize that teens will mess up, and the most important things are their safety and learning from these mistakes. ❑ NOT measure my teen's success by grades alone or compare her/his performance to siblings or classmates. Instead, I will consider her/his effort, level of ability in the specific topic, and personal improvement. ❑ Reward my teen when s/he achieves her/his goals as described in the Teen Expectations above. I realize that the success of this contract also depends on me following through with my responsibilities and promises as stated above. ❑ Read and take under serious consideration any appeal or modification request to this agreement that my teen makes in a respectful and thoughtfully composed written document.

I, ______________________________, promise to abide by the above guidelines and will willingly face the penalties we have agreed upon if I break any of them. In all cases of disagreement, my parent(s) have the authority to make the final decision. I have the right to appeal any decision or request modifications to this agreement in a respectful and thoughtfully composed written document, which will be reviewed by my parent(s), but will not guarantee a change.

______________________________ ____________________

Teen's Signature Date

I/we, the parent(s), agree to review the terms of this contract on or before ______________<date>, with my teenager ______________________, and update it to reflect newly earned privileges and responsibilities, as appropriate. I understand that school can be very tough and that my teen may not be successful at *everything*. I will encourage her/him to find what s/he is successful at and set reasonable goals in the areas that my teen has difficulty in.

Parent's Signature	Date
Parent's Signature	Date

Household Responsibilities Agreement

This agreement defines and establishes household responsibilities and associated expectations for our teen, ______________________________ __________, as of ____________________, 20______.

Teen Responsibilities	
Daily Tasks	Task 1: Task 2: Task 3: Task 4: Task 5:
Weekly Tasks	Task 1: Task 2: Task 3: Task 4: Task 5:
Monthly Tasks	Task 1: Task 2: Task 3: Task 4: Task 5:
Seasonal Tasks	Task 1: Task 2: Task 3: Task 4: Task 5:

Honor Code	I promise to: ❑ Not tell my parent(s) that I have completed a task if I have not. ❑ Not dump my tasks on my siblings/friends/other unsuspecting victims. ❑ Tell my parents immediately if I am unable to complete a task within the given time frame, so that we can find an alternative solution. (If done early enough, this will not result in a penalty.) ❑ Tell my parents immediately if I break/damage/make a mistake, so that it can be cleaned up/fixed/replaced.
Attitude	I understand that: ❑ Chores aren't fun for anyone but are necessary to keep our home livable and pleasant, therefore I will not give my parents a bad attitude about doing my tasks in a timely fashion and to the best of my ability. ❑ My parents may ask me to perform other tasks to help with the running of the family in a way that is helpful, healthy, and pleasant for all family members.
Penalties	I promise to follow the above rules and guidelines. I understand that if I break any of these terms, I am agreeing to accept one or more of the following penalties (without argument), based on the seriousness of my infraction as determined by my parent(s): ❑ Forfeit some or all of my weekly allowance. ❑ Lose the following privilege(s) until I've completed all my responsibilities. ______________________________________ ❑ Take on the following additional chores for ______ days. ______________________________________
Rewards	I may: ❑ Earn up to $______ / week by completing the above tasks in a satisfactory and timely fashion. ❑ Earn the following privileges if I complete the above tasks ________ days in a row without reminders. ______________________________________ ❑ Earn additional compensation/privileges if I do extra tasks (especially, without being asked).

Parent Responsibilities	
Support	I promise to: ❑ Respect that my teen, ______________, is becoming a young adult and would like time to her/himself, rather than always doing chores. Therefore, I will be fair and responsible when assigning the amount, frequency and difficulty of chores. ❑ Make sure that my teen fully understands the requirements of her/his tasks. I will take the time to demonstrate exactly how the tasks should be completed, and will provide constructive feedback after completion. ❑ Supply all products and tools needed to complete the assigned chores successfully.
Compensation	I will: ❑ Pay a weekly allowance of $_______ if all tasks are completed to my satisfaction. I will pay my teen on or before every ______________ <day of the week>. ❑ Allow my teen to have the agreed-upon privileges once s/he has completed the responsibilities outlined in this contract. ❑ Reward my teen with extra compensation/privileges if additional tasks are completed or my teen goes above and beyond the responsibilities outlined in this contract.
Enforcement	I will: ❑ Deduct a reasonable amount from my teen's weekly allowance or take away a privilege if s/he does not complete the tasks as agreed upon. ❑ Provide up to ______ reminders to complete the agreed-upon tasks before enacting consequences. ❑ Read and take under serious consideration any appeal or modification request to this agreement that my teen makes in a respectful and thoughtfully composed written document.

I, ______________________________, respect that my family wants our home to be clean and clutter-free and, as an active family member living under my parent(s) roof, it is my responsibility to pull my weight by completing the tasks agreed upon above. In all cases of disagreement, my parent(s) have the authority to make the final decision. I have the right to appeal any decision or request modifications to this agreement in a respectful and thoughtfully composed written document, which will be reviewed by my parent(s), but will not guarantee a change.

_______________________________ _________________

Teen's Signature Date

I/we, the parent(s), agree to review the terms of this agreement on or before ______________<date>, with my teenager ________________________, and update it to reflect newly earned privileges and responsibilities, as appropriate.

_______________________________ _________________

Parent's Signature Date

_______________________________ _________________

Parent's Signature Date

Examples of teen-appropriate tasks

- ❑ Babysit siblings
- ❑ Bring in the mail
- ❑ Clean bathroom
- ❑ Clean litter box
- ❑ Clean pool
- ❑ Clear the table
- ❑ Do the dishes
- ❑ Dust
- ❑ Empty trash
- ❑ Feed/walk pet
- ❑ Load dishwasher
- ❑ Make family meal
- ❑ Mow lawn
- ❑ Pack lunch/es
- ❑ Put away laundry
- ❑ Put away my stuff (shoes, clothes, gadgets, etc.)
- ❑ Rake lawn
- ❑ Shovel snow
- ❑ Take recycling out
- ❑ Take trash out
- ❑ Unload dishwasher
- ❑ Vacuum
- ❑ Wash/dry laundry
- ❑ Weed garden

Internet Use Agreement

This agreement defines and establishes Internet use guidelines and associated expectations for our teen, ____,
as of ____________________, 20______.

Teen Expectations	
Usage	I will: ☐ Only access the Internet from computers located in an open area <kitchen, family room, study>. ☐ Spend a maximum of ______ minutes a day online (excluding homework). ☐ Use the Internet only for the following purposes: < Homework, research, email, social media, gaming, streaming videos> ☐ Not use the Internet o between ______ p.m. and _______ a.m. on school nights or o between ______ p.m. and _______ a.m. on non-school nights unless given permission by my parent(s).
Access	I will not visits sites that: ☐ Are for adults only. ☐ Are for dating/meeting people. ☐ Are for gambling. ☐ Are sexually explicit. ☐ Cost additional money (unless I have parental permission). ☐ Promote hate groups, violence, or illegal activity.
Safety	I promise to: ☐ Protect my privacy, which means NEVER sharing: o My full name, address/location, age, school, phone number, or other personal information to anyone whom I don't know. o My password to anyone (including friends), except my parents. ☐ Alert my parents if I am being cyber-bullied or receive suspicious or alarming messages. ☐ NEVER meet someone face to face that I meet online. ☐ Click on the back button or log off if I see something that I do not like or that I know my parents consider inappropriate.

Honor Code	I will NOT: ❑ Buy or order anything online or give out any credit card information without a parent present. ❑ Download any software without my parent(s) permission. ❑ Lie about my age to access a website. ❑ Send, forward, or respond to inappropriate, hurtful, or threatening messages, emails, images, videos, or posts. ❑ Take, send, or post any photos or videos of anyone without that person's permission. ❑ Use my computer to take pictures or video of nudity, sexually suggestive activity, violence, or other inappropriate or unlawful activity. ❑ Use the Internet to copy, download, or buy schoolwork/research papers, or cheat in any way. ❑ Withhold my passwords or access to my email, bookmarks, browsing history, and privacy settings from my parents.
Penalties	I promise to abide by the above rules and guidelines. I understand that if I break any of these terms, I am agreeing to accept one or more of the following penalties (without argument), based on the seriousness of my infraction as determined by my parent(s): ❑ Lose Internet privileges for ________ days to _________ weeks. ❑ Reduce Internet use to _____ minutes a day/homework only. ❑ Pay purchasing costs incurred. ❑ Pay up to ______ in replacement/repair costs. ❑ Write a ______ word paper about Internet safety.
Rewards	If I prove that I am a safe and responsible Internet user by following the terms of this agreement for _______ consecutive days, I may earn one of the following rewards:

Parent Expectations	
Privacy	I promise to: ❑ Respect my child's privacy when s/he is online. ❑ NOT invade my child's privacy by reading emails messages or looking through her/his browsing history or bookmarks without telling my child first. ❑ Let my teen know if I have concerns and look through her/his privacy settings with her/him.
Support	I will: ❑ Support my teen when s/he alerts me to an alarming message. ❑ Do everything that I can to teach my teen to use the Internet responsibly and safely. ❑ Sit down and talk to my teen about any mistakes that s/he makes so that we can both learn from it and move on. ❑ Alert my teen if our Internet access changes and affects her/his usage.
Enforcement	I will: ❑ Give my teen the benefit of the doubt and listen to her/his side of the story before determining the penalty. ❑ Give my teen ___ warning(s) before I enact a penalty. ❑ Match the penalty to the infraction (behavior and level of seriousness). ❑ Read and take under serious consideration any appeal or modification request to this agreement that my teen makes in a respectful and thoughtfully composed written document.

I, ____, understand that having Internet access is a privilege that I must earn by being responsible and trustworthy. I acknowledge that the above rules and guidelines are established to keep me safe and teach me how to use the Internet responsibly. I understand that this agreement may be modified at the discretion of my parent(s) based on my how well I abide by it.

________________________________ ____________________

Teen's Signature Date

I/we, the parent(s), agree to review the terms of this agreement with my teenager on or before ________________<date>, and update it to reflect any new privileges my teen has earned by consistently abiding by the above terms

____ ________________________

Parent's Signature Date

____ ________________________

Parent's Signature Date

Glossary

abstinence	The practice of not doing or having something that is wanted or enjoyable.
abuse	To treat in a harmful, injurious, or offensive way.
abuse, physical	Contact intended to cause feelings of physical pain, injury, or other physical suffering or bodily harm.
abuse, sexual	Forcing undesired sexual behavior by one person upon another. When that force is immediate, of short duration, or infrequent, it is called sexual assault. The offender is referred to as a sexual abuser.
abuse, verbal	Use of words to cause harm to the person being spoken to. This includes: shouting, insulting, intimidating, threatening, shaming, demeaning, or derogatory language.
accountable	Obligation or willingness to accept responsibility.
ADHD	Attention Deficit Hyperactivity Disorder. A neural disorder in which there are significant problems with attention, hyperactivity, or acting impulsively that's not appropriate for a person's age.
affection	A quality or feeling of liking and caring for another.
aggression	Overt or suppressed hostility, either innate or resulting from continued frustration and directed outward or against oneself usually to dominate or master.
anger	A strong feeling of displeasure and belligerence, often aroused by a perceived wrong.
anorexia	A serious eating disorder especially of young women in their teens in which an abnormal fear of weight gain leads to faulty eating habits and extreme weight loss.
anxiety	Distress or uneasiness of mind caused by fear of danger, failure or misfortune.
appreciation	Recognition and enjoyment of the good qualities of someone or something; to see someone's worth, quality, or significance.
arguing	To talk about some matter, usually with different points of view; to state the reasons for or against.

attention	Taking special care of someone or something through careful listening or watching, out of kindness or courtesy.
authority	The power to determine, adjudicate, or otherwise settle issues or disputes.
back talk	A rude or quarrelsome reply.
bisexual	Sexually responsive to both sexes.
blame	To hold responsible; find fault with.
body image	A person's feelings of the attractiveness of their own body that may be forced by others or social media.
bulimia	A serious eating disorder mainly of young women that is characterized by compulsive overeating usually followed by intentional vomiting or laxative abuse.
bully	A quarrelsome, overbearing person who habitually picks on and intimidates smaller or weaker people.
cheat	To use unfair or dishonest methods to gain an advantage.
collaborate	To work with others.
communication	The imparting or interchange of thoughts, opinions, or information by speech, writing, or signs.
consequences	The effect, result, or outcome of something occurring earlier:
constructive feedback	Evaluative information that helps to develop or improve something.
criticize	To find fault with; judge unfavorably or harshly.
curfew	A regulation requiring a person to be home at a certain prescribed time.
cutting	Purposely injuring oneself by using a sharp object to scratch or cut your skin deep enough to draw blood.
cyber-bullying	The electronic posting of mean-spirited messages about a person that's often done anonymously.
depression	A condition of general emotional dejection and withdrawal; sadness greater and more prolonged than that warranted by any objective reason.
diet	A particular selection of food, especially as designed to improve a person's physical condition or to prevent or treat a disease:

discipline	Training that corrects or strengthens positive behavior and moral character.
disrespect	Lack of respect; discourtesy; rudeness.
drug	A usually illegal substance (e.g., LSD) that affects bodily activities often in a harmful way and is taken for other than medical reasons.
dyslexia	A learning disability that is usually marked by problems in reading, spelling, and writing.
eating disorder	Any of various disorders (e.g., anorexia) characterized by severe disturbances in eating habits.
emotions	Often associated and considered reciprocally influential with mood, temperament, personality, disposition, and motivation. Seven basic emotions: anger, contempt, disgust, fear, joy, sadness, surprise.
empathy	Being aware of and sharing another person's feelings, experiences, and emotions.
encouragement	Giving someone support, confidence, or hope.
entitlement	The feeling that one has a right to be given something which others believe should be obtained through effort; unrealistic expectations of favorable treatment.
erection	Enlarged state or condition of erectile tissues or organs (e.g., the penis) when filled with blood
exercise	Physical exertion for the sake of training or improvement of health.
family	Social unit consisting of one or more adults together with the children they care for.
feelings	Emotion or emotional perception or attitude.
frenemy	Blend of "friend" and "enemy" that can refer to either an enemy pretending to be a friend or someone who really is a friend but also a rival.
friend	Person who has a strong affection for and trust in another.
guilt	Feeling of responsibility or remorse for some offense, crime, wrong, etc., whether real or imagined.
happiness	State of well-being and contentment; joy.

health	Soundness of body or mind; freedom from disease or ailment.
homosexuality	Sexual desire for people of one's own sex.
hormones	A chemical substance produced in the body that controls and regulates the activity of certain cells or organs. Essential for every activity of life, including the processes of digestion, metabolism, growth, reproduction, and mood control.
humor	The power to see or tell about the amusing or comic side of things.
hygiene	A set of practices performed for the preservation of health.
insecurity	Lack of confidence or assurance; self-doubt.
kissing	Touch with the lips as a sign of love, sexual desire, reverence, or greeting.
learning disabilities	Disorder (e.g., ADHD) usually affecting school-age children of normal or above-normal intelligence, which interferes with a person's ability to learn basic academic skills.
lecture	Long, tedious reprimand.
listening	Attending closely for the purpose of hearing and understanding.
lying	Telling false statements and untruths in an attempt to deceive.
manners	Ways of behaving with reference to polite standards.
masturbation	Self stimulation of the genitals for sexual pleasure, usually to the point of orgasm.
materialism	Tendency to attach too much importance to physical comfort and material objects, often at the expense of spiritual, intellectual, or cultural values.
menstruation	Discharge of blood, secretions, and tissue debris from the uterus for a period of days, occurring approximately every month.
misbehavior	Improper, inappropriate, or bad behavior.
moodiness	Given to frequent changes of mood; temperamental; sulky.
motivate	Provide with a reason for doing something.
nagging	Annoying or irritating (a person) with persistent fault-finding or continuous urging.

name-calling	Use of abusive names to belittle or humiliate another person.
negotiation	Mutual discussion and arrangement aimed at reaching an agreement.
obesity	Medical condition in which excess body fat has accumulated to the extent that it may have a negative effect on health, leading to reduced life expectancy and/or increased health problems.
open-ended question	Needs more than a one-word answer; requires or allows an answer that is fuller than a simple yes or no.
oral sex	Sexual activity in which the genitals of one partner are stimulated by the mouth of the other; also known as fellatio and cunnilingus.
peer	Person who is equal to another in abilities, qualifications, age, background, and social status.
peer pressure	Social pressure by members of one's peer group to take a certain action, adopt certain values, or otherwise conform in order to be accepted.
persuasion	Attempt to influence a person's beliefs, attitudes, intentions, motivations, or behaviors.
PMS	Premenstrual syndrome (PMS) is a collection of emotional symptoms, with or without physical symptoms, related to a woman's menstrual cycle.
popularity	Being liked, admired, or supported by many people.
pornography	Printed or visual material containing the explicit description or display of sexual organs or activity, intended to stimulate erotic feelings.
power struggle	Unpleasant or violent competition for power and control.
praise	Expression of approval or admiration.
prejudice	Prejudging or making a decision about a person or group of people without sufficient knowledge.
pressure	Force or influence that is difficult to avoid. May lead to anxiety and stress.
privilege	Special right, advantage, or immunity granted or available only to a particular person or group of people.

puberty	Process of physical changes by which a child's body matures into an adult body capable of sexual reproduction to enable fertilization. It is initiated by hormonal signals from the brain to the gonads: the ovaries in a girl, the testes in a boy.
rape	Crime of forcing another person through physical force, duress, or drugging to have sexual intercourse with the offender against their will. Rape committed by someone known to the victim is referred to as date rape, and is just as unlawful.
religion	Set of beliefs concerning the cause, nature, and purpose of the universe. Usually involves devotional and ritual observances, and often contains a moral code governing the conduct of human affairs.
respect	Positive feeling of esteem or deference for a person.
reward	Given in recognition of one's service, effort, or achievement:
rule	Guide or principle for conduct or action.
safe sex	Sexual activity and especially sexual intercourse in which various measures (e.g., condoms) are used to avoid disease (e.g., AIDS) transmitted by sexual contact.
sarcasm	Sharp, bitter, or cutting expression or remark.
self-esteem	Realistic respect for or favorable impression of oneself; self-respect.
self-harm	Intentional, direct injury of body tissue most often done without suicidal intentions.
sexting	Sending sexually explicit photos, images, text messages, or emails by using a cell phone or other mobile device.
sexual assault	Any sexual act in which a person is threatened, coerced, or forced to engage against their will, or any nonconsensual sexual touching of a person.
sexuality	Person's sexual orientation or preference.
shame	Painful feeling arising from the consciousness of something dishonorable, improper, ridiculous, etc., done by oneself or another:
shoplifting	Theft of goods from a retail establishment.

shyness	Feeling of apprehension, lack of comfort, or awkwardness, especially in new situations or with unfamiliar people; not wanting or able to call attention to oneself.
social media	Social interaction among people in which they create, share, or exchange information and ideas in virtual communities and networks.
social skill	Facilitate interaction and communication with others.
STDs	Any of various diseases (e.g., syphilis) that are usually transmitted by direct sexual contact and that include some (such as hepatitis) that may be contracted by other than sexual means.
stealing	Taking another person's property without that person's permission or consent, with the intent to deprive the rightful owner of it.
stereotype	An oversimplified generalization about a person or group of people without regard for individual differences. Even seemingly positive stereotypes that link a person or group to a specific positive trait can have negative consequences.
stonewalling	Refusal to communicate or cooperate.
stress	Emotional and physical way in which we respond to pressure.
substance abuse	Patterned use of a substance (e.g., alcohol) in which the user consumes the substance in amounts or with methods which are harmful to themselves or others.
suicide	Intentionally taking one's own life.
swearing	Using offensive or vulgar language.
teasing	Provoking or disturbing a person by importunity or persistent petty annoyances.
threat	Expression of intent to do harm or inflict punishment, often in retaliation.
trust	Firm belief in the character, ability, strength, integrity or truth of someone or something.
underachievement	Perform, especially academically, below the potential indicated by tests of one's mental ability or aptitude.

volunteering	Offering oneself for some service or undertaking, usually without pay.
wet dream	Spontaneous orgasm during sleep that includes ejaculation for a male, or vaginal wetness or an orgasm (or both) for a female.
yelling	Giving a loud, sharp cry.

Index

I

K

L

M

N

O

P

R

S

T

U

V

W

Y

Notes

1 https://www.dosomething.org
2 Kasser, T. (2002), *The High Price of Materialism*. MIT Press, Cambridge, MA.
3 StageofLife.com March 2013 survey
4 Bronson, P. and Merryman, A. (2009). Nurture Shock. Hachette Book Group. New York, NY.
5 *U.S. News & World Report* (http://www.usnews.com)
6 Wulf-Uwe Meyer, Waldemar Mittag, and Udo Engler, (1986) "Some Effects of Praise and Blame on Perceived Ability and Affect," *Social Cognition 4(3)*, 293-308.
7 National Center for Biotechnology Information, (2014, January), *U.S. National Library of Medicine*, The Associated Press.
8 Fredrickson, B. L. (2013, July 15). Updated Thinking on Positivity Ratios. *American Psychologist*. Advance online publication. doi: 10.1037/a0033584
9 2010 Pew survey
10 National Association of Anorexia Nervosa and Associated Disorders
11 Rader Programs
12 Juvonen, J. & Gross, F. E. (2008). Extending the school social scene?—Bullying experiences in cyberspace. *Journal of School Health*, 78, 496-505.
13 Josephson's Institute of Ethics, 2000
14 National Association of School Psychologists (http://www.nasponline.org)
15 American Academy of Pediatrics (http://www.aap.org/)
16 Kubler-Ross, E., (1969), *On Death and Dying*. Simon and Schuster. New York, NY.
17 Divorcestatistics.org
18 American Academy of Pediatrics Report
19 Lam, C.B., McHale, S.H., and Crouter, A.C. (2012). Parent–Child Shared Time From Middle Childhood to Late Adolescence: Developmental Course and Adjustment Correlates. *Child Development 83 (6)*, 2089-2103.
20 The Kinsey Report
21 National Institute of Mental Health (http://www.nimh.nih.gov)
22 JumpStart Coalition
23 Berge, J.M., MacLehose, R., Loth, K.A., Eisenberg, M., Bucchianeri, M.M., and Neumark-Sztainer, D., (2013). Parent Conversations About Healthful Eating and Weight: Associations With Adolescent Disordered Eating Behaviors. *JAMA Pediatrics 167(8)*, 746-753.

24 Sabina, C., Wolak, J., and Finkelhor, D., (2008). The Nature and Dynamics of Internet Pornography Exposures for Youth. *CyberPsychology & Behavior 11(6).*

25 Obgyn.net

26 Lytch, C.E., (2004). *Choosing Church: What Makes a Difference for Teens.* Westminster John Knox Press. Louisville, KY.

27 Centers for Disease Control and Prevention (CDC)

28 Guttmacher Institute, 2014 (http://www.guttmacher.org)

29 thenationalcampaign.org

30 Planned Parenthood (http://www.plannedparenthood.org/health-info/birth-control)

31 *The Oprah Magazine* and *Seventeen* magazine sex survey.

32 The National Campaign to Prevent Teen and Unplanned Pregnancy (http://thenationalcampaign.org)

33 Centers for Disease Control and Prevention

34 Bernstein, N., (2001). *How to Keep Your Teenager Out of Trouble and What to Do If You Can't.* Workman Publishing Company. New York, NY.

35 Ablard, L.E. and Parker, W.D. (1997). Parents' achievement goals and perfectionism in their academically talented children. *Journal of Youth & Adolescence 26,* 651-67.

36 Evans, D.L. et al. (2005), *Treating and Preventing Adolescent Mental Health Disorders.* Oxford University Press, New York, NY.

37 National Institute on Alcohol Abuse and Alcoholism

38 Madden, M., Lenhart, A., Duggan, M., Cortesi, S., and Gassert, U. (2013). Teens and Technology 2013. Pew Research Internet Project Report.

39 www.fbi.gov

40 Centers for Disease Control and Prevention

41 Louis Harris and Associates study

42 Based on the Tanner scale (also known as the Tanner stages)

43 https://ink.niche.com/

Additional Resources

Achor, S. (2010). The Happiness Advantage: The Seven Principles of Positive Psychology That Fuel Success and Performance at Work. Crown Business.

American Psychological Association (2014). Controlling Anger—Before It Controls You. http://www.apa.org/topics/anger/control.aspx#

Association for Psychological Science, (2012), Want to limit aggression? Practice self-control. *Science Daily*.

Babbitt, E.F. (2012). *International Negotiation and Conflict Resolution*. The Fletcher School of Law and Diplomacy. Tufts University. Program on Negotiation.

Backus, W.D. and Backus, C. (1992). *Empowering Parents: How to Raise Obedient Children—It's Possible, It's Right*. Bethany House Publishing. Ada, MI.

Branden, N. (1969). *The Psychology of Self-Esteem*. Bantam Books. New York, NY.

Brown, B. (2012) *Daring Greatly: How the Courage to Be Vulnerable Transforms the Way We Live, Love, Parent, and Lead*. Gotham. New York, NY.

Brown, B. B. & Klute, C. (2006). Friendships, cliques, and crowds. In G. R. Adams & M. D. Berzonsky (Eds.). *Blackwell Handbook of Adolescence*, 330-348. Blackwell Publishing. Malden, MA.

Carter, C. (2011). *Raising Happiness: 10 Simple Steps For More Joyful Kids and Happier Parents*. Ballantine Books. New York, NY.

Chapman, G.D. (2010). *The 5 Love Languages of Teenagers New Edition: The Secret to Loving Teens Effectively*. Northfield Publishing. Chicago, IL.

Clark, C. (2011). *Hurt 2.0. inside the world of today's TEENAGERS*. Baker Academic, Grand Rapids, MI.

Clark, L. (1998). *SOS Help for Emotions. Managing Anxiety, Anger & Depression*. Parents Press. Bowling Green, KY.

Covey, S. (1998). *The 7 Habits of Highly Effective Teens: The Ultimate Teenage Success Guide*. Fireside. New York, NY.

Cuddy, A. (2012). Your Body Language Shapes Who You Are. TedGlobal 2012. http://www.ted.com/talks/amy_cuddy_your_body_language_shapes_who_you_are

Dale Carnegie Training (2009). *The 5 Essential People Skills: How to Assert Yourself, Listen to Others, and Resolve Conflicts*. Touchstone Publishing. New York, NY.

Darling, N., Cumsille, P., Caldwell, L.L., and Dowdy, B. (2006). 'Predictors of Adolescents' Disclosure to Parents and Perceived Parental Knowledge: Between- and Within-Person Differences. *Journal of Youth and Adolescence, 35 (4)*, 659-670.

Doe, M. and Walch, M. (1998). *10 Principles for Spiritual Parenting.* Harper Perennial, New York, NY.

Dweck, C.S. (2006). *Mindset. The New Psychology of Success.* Ballantine Books. New York, NY.

Ekman, P. (2003). *Emotions Revealed. Recognizing Faces and Feelings to Improve Communication and Emotional Life.* Henry Holt and Company. New York, NY.

Faber, A. and Mazlish, E. (2006) *How to Talk So Teens Will Listen and Listen So Teens Will Talk.* William Morrow Paperbacks. New York, NY.

Feinstein, S.G. (2009) *Secrets of the Teenage Brain.* Skyhorse Publishing. New York, NY.

Fisher, R., Ury, W., Patton, B. (2011). *Getting to Yes: Negotiating Agreement Without Giving In.* Penguin Books. New York, NY.

Ginsburg, K. and FitzGerald, S. (2011). *Letting Go with Love and Confidence: Raising Responsible, Resilient, Self-Sufficient Teens in the 21st Century.* Avery Trade. New York, NY.

Goleman, D. (1994). *Emotional Intelligence. Why It Can Matter More Than IQ.* Bantam Books. New York, NY.

Grotevant, H. (1997). Adolescent development in family contexts. In N. Eisenberg (Ed.), *Handbook of child psychology* (5th ed.), Social, emotional, and personality development, 1097–1149. Wiley. New York, NY.

Guarendi, R. (2007). Good Discipline, Great Teens. Servant Books. Cincinnati, OH.

Hemmen, L. (2012). *Parenting a Teen Girl: A Crash Course on Conflict, Communication and Connection with Your Teenage Daughter.* New Harbinger Publications. Oakland, CA.

Holmes, T.R., Bond, L.A. and Byrne, C. (2008). Mothers' Beliefs about Knowledge and Mother-Adolescent Conflict. *Journal of Social and Personal Relationships, 25(4)*, 561-586.

Kindlon, D. and Thompson, M. (2000). Raising Cain: Protecting the Emotional Life of Boys. Ballantine Books. New York, NY.

Kohlberg, L. (1970). Moral development and the education of adolescents. In R.F. Purnell, ed., *Adolescents and the American High School.* Hold, Rinehart & Winston. New York, NY.

Leman, K. (2012). Have a New Teenager by Friday: How to Change Your Child's Attitude, Behavior & Character in 5 Days. Revell; Reprint edition. Ada, MI.

Lerner, J.V., Rosenberg, R., Lerner, M. (eds) (2001). *Adolescence in America: An Encyclopedia.* Santa Barbara, CA.

Levine, M. (2008). *The Price of Privilege*. Harper, New York, NY.

Markham, L. (2012). *Peaceful Parent, Happy Kids. How to Stop Yelling and Start Connecting*. Penguin Group. New York, NY.

Meyer, P. (2010). *Liespotting: Proven Techniques to Detect Deception*. St. Martin's Press. New York, NY.

Meyer, P. (2011, July). *How to Spot a Liar*. Presented at TEDGlobal 2011.

Miller, J.G. (2004). *QBQ! The Question Behind the Question: Practicing Personal Accountability at Work and in Life*. Putnam. New York, NY.

Mozes, A. (2013). Screaming, Cursing at Your Misbehaving Teen May Backfire

Murnighan, J.K. (2012). *Do Nothing. How to Stop Overmanaging and Become a Great Leader*. Portfolio Hardcover. New York, NY.

National Institute of Mental Health (2011). The Teen Brain: Still Under Construction. *NIH Publication(11)*, 4929.

Nelsen, J. and Lott, L. (2012). *Positive Discipline for Teenagers, Revised 3rd Edition: Empowering Your Teens and Yourself Through Kind and Firm Parenting*. Harmony. New York, NY.

Pipher, M. (1994). *Reviving Ophelia. Saving the Selves of Adolescent Girls*. Ballantine Books. New York, NY.

Powell, M. (2013). *Mind Games*. Sterling Publishing Company, Inc. New York, NY.

Rice, P., & Dolgin, K.G. (2002). *Adolescent: Development, relationships, and culture (10th ed.)*. Allyn & Bacon. Needham Heights, MA.

Rosemond, J. (2012). Parent-Babble: How Parents Can Recover from Fifty Years of Bad Expert Advice. Andrews McMeel Publishing. Riverside, NJ.

Runkel, E. (2008). *Screamfree Parenting: The Revolutionary Approach to Raising Your Kids by Keeping Your Cool*. Harmony. New York, NY.

Sanavi, F. S., Baghbanian, A., Shovey, M.F. and Ansari-Moghaddam, A. (2013). A study on family communication pattern and parenting styles with quality of life in adolescent. *Journal of Pakistan Medical Association 63(11)*.

Santrock, J.W. (2003). *Adolescence*. McGraw-Hill. New York, NY.

Santrock, J.W. (2012). *Life-Span Development, 14th Ed*. McGraw-Hill. New York, NY.

Siegler, D.J. (2014). *Brainstorm: The Power and Purpose of the Teenage Brain*. Scribe Publications. Royal Oak, MI.

Steinberg, L. (2001). We know some things: Adolescent-parent relationships in retrospect and prospect. *Journal of Research on Adolescence, 11*, 1–19.

Steinberg, L. (2004). *The 10 Basic Principles of Good Parenting. Simon & Schuster*. New York, NY.

Steinberg, L. (2008). *Adolescence, 8th ed.* McGraw-Hill. New York, NY.

Study found verbal abuse promoted more disobedience and conflict. *U.S. News & World Report.*

Swink, D.F. (2013). I Don't Feel Your Pain: Overcoming Roadblocks to Empathy. Threat Management. *Psychology Today.*

Ury, W. (2007). *The Power of a Positive No: Save The Deal Save The Relationship and Still Say No.* Bantam. New York, NY.

Van Petten, V. (2011). *Do I Get My Allowance Before or After I'm Grounded?: Stop Fighting, Start Talking, and Get to Know Your Teen.* Plume. New York, NY.

Walsh, D. (2005). *Why Do They Act That Way?: A Survival Guide to the Adolescent Brain for You and Your Teen.* Atria Books. New York, NY.

White, A.M. and Swartzwelder, S. (2013). *What Are They Thinking?!: The Straight Facts about the Risk-Taking, Social-Networking, Still-Developing Teen Brain.* W. W. Norton & Company. New York, NY.

Wiseman, R. (2002). *Queen Bees & Wannabes. Helping Your Daughter Survive Cliques, Gossip, Boyfriends & Other Realities of Adolescence.* Three Rivers Press. New York. NY

Wolf, A. (2011). *I'd Listen to My Parents If They'd Just Shut Up: What to Say and Not Say When Parenting Teens.* William Morrow Paperbacks. New York, NY.

About the Author

Dr. Cameron Caswell is a family coach, author, public speaker, and teacher. She is also the founder of Fuel Center, LLC, which specializes in helping parents and teens learn to live together in harmony by redefining their relationships, rebuilding mutual respect and trust, and developing a deeper understanding of one another. Dr. Caswell lives in Northern Virginia with her daughter, Alexa, who has promised that she will *not* become a "crazy teen" when she gets older. Dr. Caswell is *not* holding her breath. Learn more at www.theFuelCenter.com.